Strategic Paper E3
Enterprise Strategy

First edition 2009
Fourth edition 2012

ISBN 9781 4453 9449 7 (Previous ISBN 9780 7517 9586 8)

e-Book ISBN 9781 4453 9270 7

British Library Cataloguing-in-Publication Data

A catalogue record for this book is available from the British Library

Published by BPP Learning Media Ltd, BPP House, Aldine Place, London W12 8AA

www.bpp.com/learningmedia

Printed in the United Kingdom

Your learning materials, published by BPP Learning Media Ltd,
are printed on paper sourced from sustainable, managed forests.

Welcome to BPP Learning Media's CIMA **Passcards** for **Strategic Paper E3 Enterprise Strategy.**

- They **focus on your exam** and **save you time**.

- They incorporate **diagrams** to kick start your memory.

- They follow the overall **structure** of the BPP Learning Media Study Texts, but BPP Learning Media's CIMA **Passcards** are not just a condensed book. Each card has been separately designed for clear presentation. Topics are self-contained and can be grasped visually.

- CIMA **Passcards** are still **just the right size** for pockets, briefcases and bags.

- CIMA **Passcards** should be used in conjunction with the question plan in the front pages of the Kit. The plan identifies key questions for you to try in the Kit.

Run through the **Passcards** as often as you can during your final revision period. The day before the exam, try to go through the **Passcards** again! You will then be well on your way to passing your exams.

Good luck!

Contents

Introduction chapter: key strategic models

Topic List

Key strategic models

Paper E3 builds on knowledge acquired in E1 and E2, which includes a number of models that can be used in strategic management and assessing the competitive environment.

These models (such as Porter's five forces and his diamond model) are therefore assumed knowledge in the E3 exam, so they could be tested in the context of a scenario question even though they are not specifically referred to in the E3 syllabus.

The following models are considered to be assumed knowledge at E3. If you are not familiar with them, refer to the E2 study text and passcards to ensure you could apply them in your E3 exam if necessary.

- PEST (PESTEL) analysis

- SWOT analysis

- Stakeholder mapping (Mendelow's matrix)

- Porter's diamond

- Porter's five forces (threat of new entrants, threat of substitutes, bargaining power of customers, bargaining power of suppliers, industry rivalry)

- Competitor analysis

- Competitive strategies (generic strategies)

1: Business strategy and strategy development

Topic List

Strategic planning

The rational model

Other approaches to strategy

Management accounting and business strategy

Management accounting systems

Strategic role of directors

There are a number of different approaches to strategic planning, as well as a range of different interpretations about how organisations can best implement their strategies.

It is important to consider strategy in the context of an organisation's history and culture, its resources, and its competitive environment.

Planning

is the establishment of objectives, and the formulation, evaluation and selection of the policies, strategies, tactics and action required to achieve those objectives.

is the basis for:

- Position-based approach
- Resource-based approach

Managing business strategy

Strategy:	course of action to achieve a specific objective
Strategic plan:	statement of long term goals, and those policies which will ensure their achievement
Strategic management:	management of the elements involved in planning and controlling a business strategy
Tactics:	the short term plan for achieving an entity's objectives

Advantages and Disadvantages of the rational model

Advantages	Disadvantages
■ Identifies risks	■ Not proven to bring advantage
■ Forces managers to think	■ May become over-formal and reduce initiative
■ Forces decision-making	■ Assumes internal politics do not exist
■ Formal targets enable control	■ Assumes managers know everything
■ Enforces organisational coherence and co-ordination	■ Separates planning from doing
	■ Cannot cope with shocks and discontinuities

The rational model of strategic planning

Strategic analysis

Mission
- Purpose
- Policies
- Competences
- Products
- Values
- Culture

Vision and strategic intent
Where the organisation wants to be

Goals
- Stakeholder expectations

Objectives
- Quantified measures

Environmental analysis
Opportunities and threats
- PEST/PESTEL
- Porter's 5 Forces
- Scenarios

Corporate appraisal
- SWOT analysis
- Gap analysis

Position audit
Strengths and weaknesses
- Resources, competences
- Value chain
- Systems structure
- Portfolio analysis

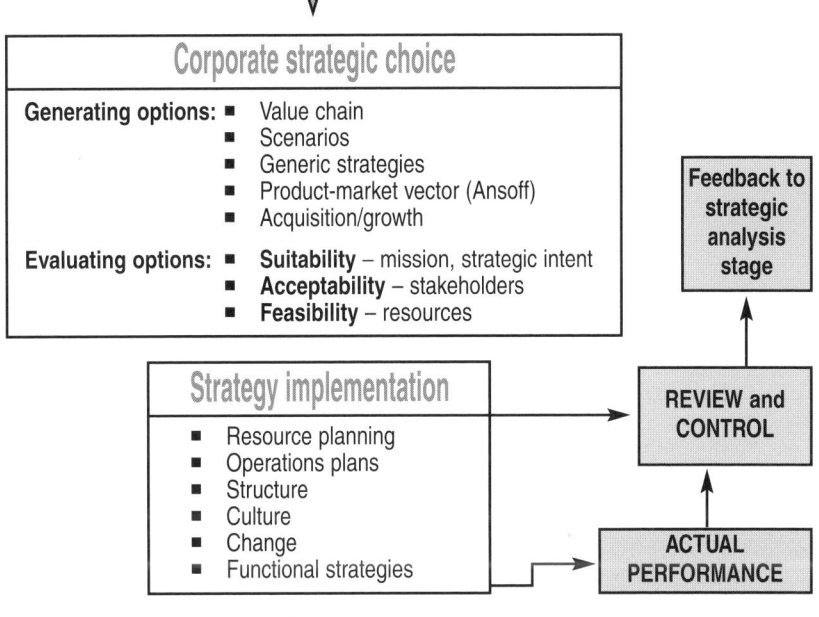

Instead of showing strategic management as a linear process (like the rational model does) Johnson, Scholes & Whittington emphasise the interrelationships between analysis, choice and implementation, and the way the three elements are interdependent. In particular, note the importance of implementation in delivering a strategy.

There have been many proposals for alternatives to the rational model, most emphasising creativity and pragmatism.

Alternatives

- Freewheeling opportunism
- Bounded rationality
- Incrementalism
- Emergent strategies

Freewheeling opportunism

– 'seize opportunities as they arise'

- Flexible and creative?
- Undisciplined and unco-ordinated?
- Reacting rather than acting?

Bounded rationality

Strategic managers' decision making is constrained by the time and amount of information available to them and by their own skills, habits and awareness.

 They:

- Do not consider all options, but choose from a restricted range
- Make political compromises by partisan mutual adjustment
- Satisfice rather than optimise

Incrementalism

Development by small scale extensions of past practices.

 This approach avoids major errors by the exercise of caution and produces acceptable solutions because it uses consultation, compromise and accommodation.

Logical incrementalism combines this approach with an in-depth review to establish the broad outlines of strategy.

1: Business strategy and strategy development

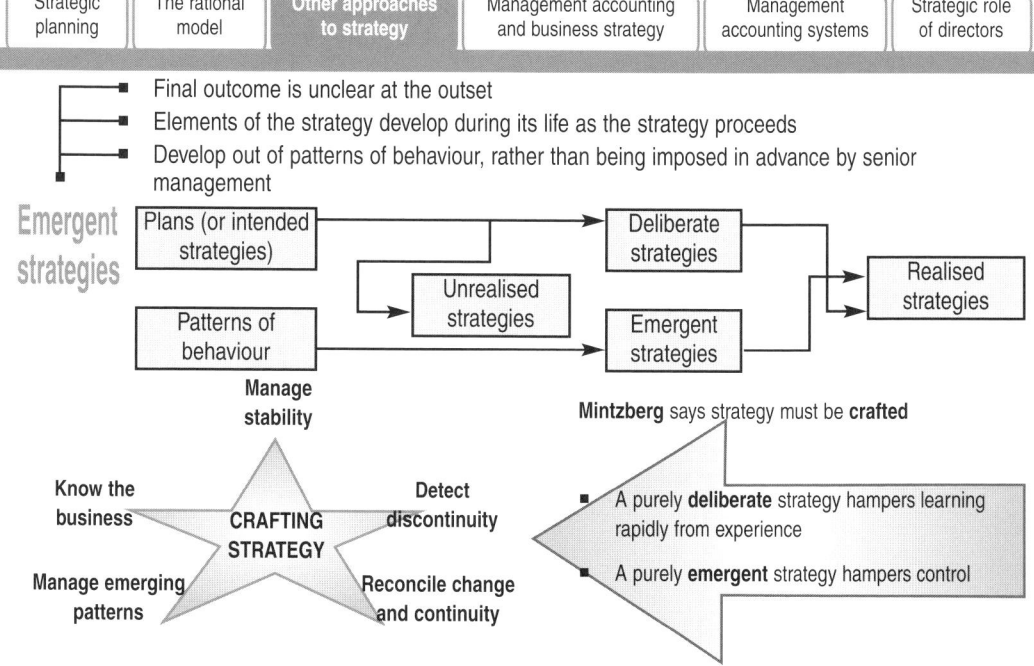

- Final outcome is unclear at the outset
- Elements of the strategy develop during its life as the strategy proceeds
- Develop out of patterns of behaviour, rather than being imposed in advance by senior management

Emergent strategies

Plans (or intended strategies) → Deliberate strategies

Unrealised strategies

Patterns of behaviour → Emergent strategies

Deliberate strategies → Realised strategies
Emergent strategies → Realised strategies

Manage stability

CRAFTING STRATEGY
- Know the business
- Detect discontinuity
- Manage emerging patterns
- Reconcile change and continuity

Mintzberg says strategy must be **crafted**

- A purely **deliberate** strategy hampers learning rapidly from experience
- A purely **emergent** strategy hampers control

Chaos Theory – *Stacey*

Organisations as systems exhibit **bounded instability**, operating at the chaotic interface between predictability and randomness.

They function through self-organising **complex responsive processes** based on **informal interaction** rather than the traditional **cybernetic** approach.

Cybernetic approach depends on well established objectives and a reasonably predictable environment.

Complex informal approach can respond to new situations by generating rapid, far-reaching change using spontaneously generated mechanisms such as *ad hoc* committees and short cuts through inappropriate procedures. Managers are not external controllers, they are embedded in the system's 'self-organising conversational life', which is fundamental to the way the organisation works.

Chaos theory also highlights that organisations are likely to oscillate between periods of relative stability and states of flux (periods of turbulence which will lead to a new order emerging.)

Resource-based strategy

Positioning strategies (eg the rational model) seek to develop and maintain competitive advantage by responding to the threats and opportunities in the competitive environment.

The **resource-based view** is that *sustainable* competitive advantage can only come from the **possession of unique resources** (or **competences**) within an organisation because:

- The business environment is too complex and dynamic for effective analysis and response.
- Competitors will rapidly imitate any position-based strategy.

Resources

Protected intellectual property – designs, processes, copyrights

Scarce raw materials, unique production or distribution facilities

Competences

Such as: experience – talent – management – techniques

Johnson, Scholes & Whittington say:

Threshold level of competence required in all activities.

Core competences out perform competitors and are difficult to imitate.

Hamel & Prahalad say core competences have three qualities:

- **Disproportionate contribution** to value customer receives
- **'Competitively unique'**
  - actually unique
  - superior to competitors
  - can be dramatically improved
- **Extendable** to new products

Strategy

'A course of action, including the specification of resources required, to achieve a specific objective'.

Strategic management accounting (SMA)

'A form of management accounting in which emphasis is placed on information which relates to factors **external** to the firm as well as **non-financial information** and internally generated information.'

Key issues for SMA

- External orientation
- Future orientation
- Goal congruence

Information requirements for SMA

- Competitors' costs
- Product/customer profitability
- Product pricing
- The value of market share

- Effect of aquisitions/ mergers
- Capacity expansion
- Entry or exit decisions
- Shareholder wealth

Exam focus

Most strategic decisions are unique, so the information needed is likely to be ad hoc and specially tailored. Any strategies you recommend in your exam must be tailored specifically to the scenario given in the question.

The successful SMA system must bridge a gap.

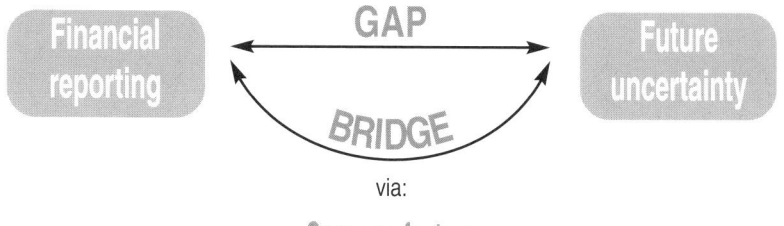

via:

Success factors

- Aid strategic decisions – close the communication gap between accountants and managers
- Identify the type of decision – and offer performance measures
- Distinguish between economic and managerial performance
- Provide relevant information – distinguish committed, discretionary and engineered costs
- Use standard costs strategically
- Allow for changes over time

3 purposes for information from management accounting systems

1 Strategic planning

- Information about the environment (PESTEL, market size/market growth)
- Internal data (eg profitability, cost of funds, investment requirements)

2 Management control

All the processes used by managers to ensure that organisational goals are achieved and procedures adhered to, and that the organisation responds appropriately to changes in the environment.

Information

The information required embraces the entire organisation and provides a comparison between actual results and the plan.

3 Operational control

Information needed to conduct day-to-day implementation of plans - largely details of individual transactions

1: Business strategy and strategy development

Good corporate governance

- Risk management and reduction
- Internal control
- Accountability to shareholders and other stakeholders, and dialogue with them
- Conducting a business in an ethical/effective way
- Good supervision to enhance performance
- Applying the spirit of the law

Role of the board

- Leadership
- Policy/strategic decisions
- Performance assessed
- Mix of skills/expertise
- Formal procedures
- Acquisitions/disposals
- Capital projects
- Treasury management

But need to consider what aspects of strategy development are directors' responsibilities compared to managers' responsibilities.

Directors' accountability to a range of stakeholders highlights the importance of stakeholder management, and it also highlights the increasing importance of ethics and corporate social responsibility within business strategy.

2: Stakeholders and corporate objectives

Topic List

Mission

Goals and objectives

Stakeholder management

Social responsibility

Not for profit and the public sector

Differing corporate frameworks have differing objectives. Businesses generally pursue some kind of financial return, but organisations often face competing objectives that may conflict with one another.

Equally, managing the expectations of different groups of stakeholders can also be an essential part of strategic planning.

Mission is the logical starting point of the process of strategy.

Mission

The entity's fundamental objectives, expressed in general terms.

Includes, typically:

- Purpose
- Basic strategy eg products
- Policies and standards of behaviour
- Values and culture
  - business principles
  - internal relationships
  - behaviour

A formal **mission statement** may:

- Impress customers
- Motivate staff
- Guide manager's actions
- Guide strategic thinking

Resource planning

This involves:

- Establishing currently obtainable resources
- Estimating the resources needed
- Assigning management responsibility
- Identifying factors affecting resource availability

BUT a mission statement may also:

- Be ignored in practice
- Be treated cynically as mere PR
- Merely rationalise what is done anyway
- Be the same as everyone else's

→ **The organisation must know what it wants to achieve.**

Mission statements are open-ended, so in order to implement its strategy and manage performance, an organisation needs to develop some more specific objectives and targets.

Goals and Objectives

Goals and objectives flow from mission.

They should be:
- **S**pecific
- **M**easurable
- **A**chievable (or Agreed)
- **R**elevant (or Realistic)
- **T**ime bound

They should balance:
- Long term considerations
- Short term imperatives
- Conflicting objectives

- They should be **consistent** across the organisation so that all pull together

- Operational goals can be measured

- Non-operational goals cannot be measured

The hierarchy of objectives

| Corporate objectives for the firm as a whole | determine | Unit objectives for individual departments |

| Primary objectives | should take precedence over | Secondary objectives |

2: Stakeholders and corporate objectives

It is not always easy to identify the primary objective.

Commercial and financial goals

Profitability
ROCE/ROI
EPS

£

Dividends
Market value of shares

Most companies pursue several objectives simultaneously. They might seek innovation, increased market share, productivity, survival, quality and customer satisfaction.

(They also need to consider social responsibility objectives.)

Short termism

is a tendency to place pressure and emphasis on the achievement of results in the near future, rather than in the medium or longer term.

TRADE ↓ OFFS

Examples

Long term	Short term
R&D expenditure needed for company development	→ Cut it back to increase short-term profits
Advertising to maintain market share	→ Sacrifice this spend to preserve liquidity

In a **hierarchy of objectives**, the highest level of objective for a commercial organisation will always be based on **profitability** over the long term, though **growth** may be regarded as of equal importance.

Secondary objectives include functional and departmental objectives as well as corporate objectives that support the main objective.

Example	
Corporate objective:	Profit improvement
Supporting objectives:	Cut administrative costs
	Improve quality
Despatch dept objective:	reduce misdeliveries to 3% of total

Conflict between the demands of secondary objectives can be dealt with by:

- Rational evaluation
- **Bargaining** between managers
- **Satisficing** ie satisfactory rather than ideal performance
- **Sequential attention** to goals in turn
- **Priority setting** by senior managers
- Exercise of power

Stakeholders

Those persons and organisations that have a legitimate interest in the strategy of the organisation.

Stakeholders	Possible interests
Managers; employees	Careers; salaries, promotion; benefits; job security; job satisfaction
Shareholders	Shareholder wealth; capital growth; profitability, dividends
Bankers	Repayment of loans; security of loans
Suppliers	Profitable sales; payment for goods and services; long term relationship
Customers	Value for money; product/services as ordered; quality of service; competitive price
Government	Jobs, taxes, impact on local economy/community, national competitiveness
Pressure groups	Pollution, human rights, environmental (green) issues
Unions	Members' rights

Organisations have many stakeholders, with lots of different interests. This can lead to stakeholder conflict.

A firm can make strategic gains by managing stakeholder relationships.

 Can create positive, productive, long-lasting relationships

BUT, if stakeholders are mis-managed, can damage relationship and cause threats, eg withdrawal of resources, lost customers, reputational damage

Such opportunities and threats should be analysed in terms of

- Impact
- Direction
- Time scale
- Ability to resolve

The way organisations respond to external pressures is a key part of strategic management.

Corporate political activity, such as lobbying, election funding, petitions and coalition building is potentially an important aspect of stakeholder management, with government being the stakeholder in question. Corporate political activity represents attempts to influence government decisions in a way that is favourable to the economic survival and success of an organisation or an industry.

Corporate social responsibility (CSR) is an organisation's obligation to maximise positive stakeholders benefits while minimising the negative effects of its actions.

Should businesses actively practise social responsibility?

Examples

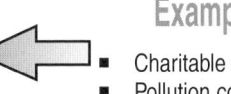

The business as fixer of social problems

- Charitable donations
- Pollution control
- Community activities

Big business has the resources to fight inequalities

BUT

Companies already discharge their responsibilities by contributing towards tax revenues

The social audit recognises the expectations on a firm to promote social responsibility. In addition, there are 'green' pressures.

- Pressure groups
- Employees
- Legislation

- Environmental screening
- Sustainability of resources
- Ecological concerns

Long term
v
Short term

2: Stakeholders and corporate objectives

Environmental concerns

Sustainability

Sustainable activity uses resources no faster than they can be replaced, and waste emissions are held down to a level that the environment can absorb.

Elkington suggests sustainability should be measured by a '**triple bottom line**'

> **Economic prosperity**
> **Environmental quality**
> **Social justice**

Environmental management accounting enhances the internal control and reporting system to promote both economic and environmental efficiency.

- Life cycle assessments of environmental impact
- Costs of undesirable outputs such as waste and noise
- Risk assessments include environmental impact
- Waste minimisation in production processes

The impact of green issues

- Demand for environmentally friendly products
- Public concern and action about pollution, habitat destruction and global warming
- Government action through regulation and taxation
- Impact of bad publicity (or chance to exploit environmental friendliness as a marketing tool)

But

- Limit to consumer willingness to change lifestyles (or to pay more for sustainable products)
- Cynicism about 'green' claims
- Public ignorance of actual economic and environmental impacts of 'green' policies

Sustainability and strategy: Strategic decision-makers need to incorporate longer-term issues with short-term ones. If they focus too much on short-term issues this could undermine an organisation's longer-term reputation and prospects.

Possible issues relating to sustainability and triple bottom line

Environmental quality	Social justice	Economic prosperity
<ul><li>Resource usage and use of renewable resources</li><li>Contamination</li><li>Levels of waste</li><li>CO_2 emissions</li><li>Use of locally sourced inputs to reduce carbon footprint</li><li>Relationship with authorities (eg to secure planning permission)</li></ul>	<ul><li>Being seen as an attractive employer</li><li>Working conditions</li><li>Labour practices (eg health and safety; training; equal opportunities)</li><li>Human rights</li><li>Contribution to local community (eg through sponsorships)</li><li>Product responsibility (eg health and safety for consumers; ethical consumerism)</li></ul>	<ul><li>Business relations (eg with banks and shareholders</li><li>Relationships with customers and suppliers</li><li>Market position</li><li>Brand name (eg potential damage to sales from negative publicity)</li></ul>

Ethics

Business ethics and CSR are not the same thing – behaving ethically is only one part of the CSR.

But remember the five fundamental principles in CIMA's Ethical code:

1   Integrity

2   Objectivity

3   Professional competence and due care

4   Confidentiality

5   Professional behaviour

If one or more of these principles is threatened in an organisation, this could create an **ethical dilemma** for the management accountant in that organisation.

A professional accountant may be required to **resolve a conflict** in relation to compliance with the fundamental principles.

Need to be aware of the potential **threats** a management accountant could face ...

... and the **safeguards** in place to mitigate against those threats

Efficiency is a key objective in 'not for profit' and public sector organisations, due to the limited amount of resources available. These resources often determine the strategy adopted.

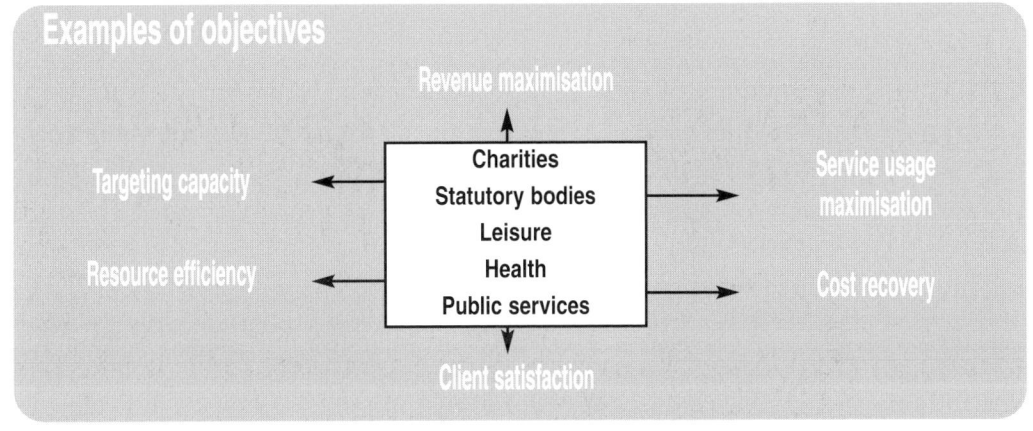

Examples of objectives

Revenue maximisation

Targeting capacity

Resource efficiency

Charities
Statutory bodies
Leisure
Health
Public services

Service usage maximisation

Cost recovery

Client satisfaction

Notes

3: Strategic decision making

The influences of the environment on an organisation are very important, and environmental changes might have an impact on corporate appraisal. However, information about the environment is often uncertain and incomplete. This means strategic decision is a complicated process.

One important approach to choosing a strategy is seeking a good fit with the environment.

The impact of uncertainty

Complexity + dynamism = uncertainty:

Complexity

- Variety of influences
- Interconnectedness of influences

Dynamism

- Pace of change

High uncertainty leads to:

- Desire for more **information**
- **Conservative** strategy with some **emergent** strategy
- Shorter planning time horizon

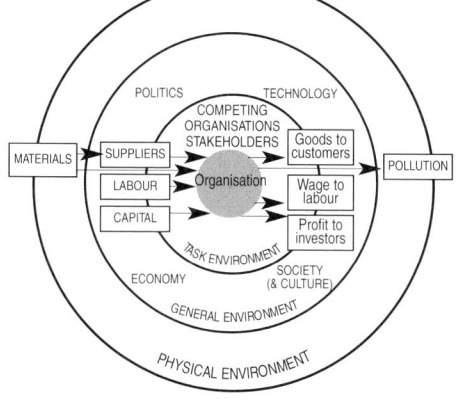

Strategic intelligence

is what a firm needs to know about its environment to enable it to anticipate change and design appropriate strategies.

Creating strategic intelligence

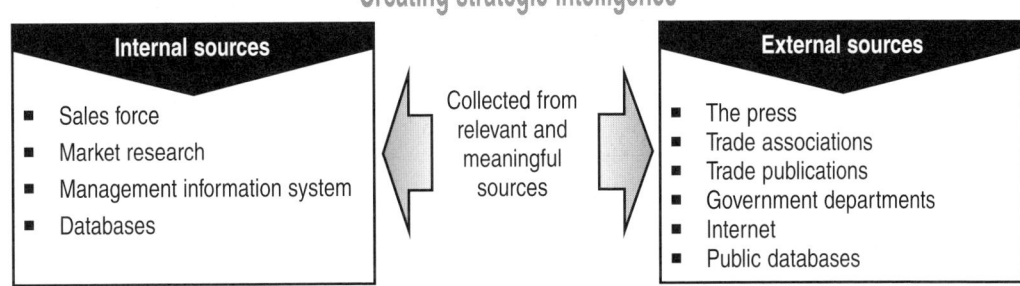

Internal sources

- Sales force
- Market research
- Management information system
- Databases

Collected from relevant and meaningful sources

External sources

- The press
- Trade associations
- Trade publications
- Government departments
- Internet
- Public databases

After the information has been collected, it needs to be organised, analysed, communicated and finally used as strategic intelligence.

One of the ways organisations can allow for uncertainty in their strategic decision making is by making use of real options.

1 **The option to make follow-on investments**

A project may not make a positive return by itself, but it may open up other potentially lucrative projects which an organisation can then take advantage of.

2 **The option to abandon a project**

If the actual revenue streams from a project turn out to be lower than expected, the option to abandon a project would be valuable to an organisation.

3 **The option to wait**

An organisation's decision making could be improved by waiting and being able to take advantage of new information which might become available. So, the option to 'wait and see' before making a decision could be valuable to an organisation.

Gap analysis

is a comparison between **desired future position** and a **forecast** based on continuing current activities and strategies.

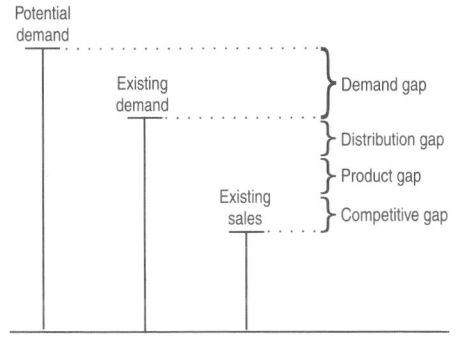

The **demand gap** is the difference between total market potential and current demand from users.

The **distribution gap**, **product gap** and **competitive gap** together make up the difference between current demand and actual sales achieved.

(a) The **distribution gap** arises from lack of access to or utilisation of distribution channels.

(b) The **product gap** arises from product failure or deliberate product decisions.

(c) The **competitive gap** arises from failures of pricing or promotion.

> The term is commonly used of a gap in overall performance: that is profitability

The profit gap is the difference between the target profits and the forecast profits.

(a) First of all the firm can estimate the effects on the gap of any projects or strategies in the pipeline. Some of the gap might be filled by a new project.

(b) Then, if a gap remains, new strategies have to be considered to close the gap:

- Improved efficiency
- Growth (new products, new markets, or both)

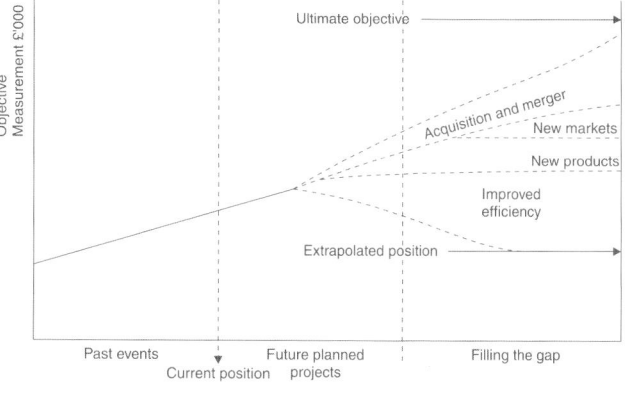

Forecast:

is 'a prediction of future events and their quantification for planning purposes'.

Projection:

is 'an expected future trend pattern obtained by extrapolation. It is principally concerned with quantitative factors whereas a forecast includes judgements.'
(CIMA Official Terminology)

- When size and timing of cash flows can be forecast with accuracy, NPV can be used
- Projects repeated several times can be assessed using expected values and decision trees
- Time series analysis shows the degree of correlation between two variables
- Econometric leading indicators indicate the future, but with uncertain lag

Consensus forecasts

Jury forecasts combine a range of expert opinion but personality and group dynamics can reduce their usefulness.

Delphi technique combines experts' opinions anonymously and iteratively to avoid the problems mentioned above.

Experts tend to be over-optimistic.

Think tank: a group of experts is encouraged to speculate about future developments in particular areas, and to identify possible causes of action.

Brainstorming: a group of people from across an organisation generate ideas without any initial evaluation or criticism of them. Once the list of ideas is complete, then they begin to be evaluated.

Scenario planning

A scenario is an internally consistent view of what the future might turn out to be based on sets of key drivers for change. Scenario planning is a way of dealing with possible major or discontinuous changes in the environment.

Macro scenarios	**Industry scenarios**
Developed by global organisations (eg energy companies)	Relate to a specific industry
■ Identify drivers of change - 10 year horizon	■ Outline a number of uncertainties
■ Discern patterns and trends and combine into a viable framework	■ Identify what causes the uncertainties
■ Create mini scenarios (say, 7-10)	■ Make assumptions about each cause
■ Group into 2 or 3 wider scenarios	■ Combine assumptions into scenario
■ Debate and test for coherence and probability	■ Predict industry structure in each scenario
■ Identify critical issues arising	■ Identify sources of competitive advantage
	■ Identify competitive behaviour in each scenario and the competences or capabilities needed to be successful in each scenario.

Jury forecasts, the Delphi technique and scenario planning are all ways management can attempt to get insights into the future and prepare for some of the opportunities and threats which may arise.

(Remember foresight and forecasting are very different concepts though).

4 stages of a foresight project	Possible foresight techniques
<ul><li>Monitoring – identifying relevant current trends</li><li>Analysis – understanding drivers of change</li><li>Projection – anticipating what might happen in the future</li><li>Transformation – drawing implications for the business of the possible projected futures</li></ul>	<ul><li>Scenario planning</li><li>Delphi technique</li><li>Jury forecasts</li><li>Cross-impact analysis</li><li>Morphological analysis</li><li>Visioning</li><li>Opportunity mapping</li><li>Trend extrapolation</li></ul>

Remember, one of the disadvantages of foresight is that it relies on the future being shaped by actions which can be imagined now.

3: Strategic decision making

The whole logic of scenario planning and foresight reminds us that the future is uncertain. Part of this uncertainty comes from not knowing how **competitors** will react to new strategies introduced by an organisation.

Game theory shows that an organisation cannot develop its own strategy without considering the possible reactions of its competitors. Competitors' reactions may mean the outcomes of a strategy are very different to that intended, such that the strategy may benefit neither the firm nor its competitors.

Strategy should be treated as an interaction between the firm and its competitors.

Organisation

- Current position in environment
- Internal resources

STRATEGY

Competitors

- How will they react?

Game theory also suggests that it may benefit firms to **co-operate** and **negotiate** with others in the search for optimal solutions rather than working alone and competing with all the other players in a market. This helps explain the rationale for **strategic alliances** or joint ventures.

4: Resource audit

Topic List

Position and resource audits

Value chain analysis

Supply chain management

The product portfolio

New product development

Benchmarking

The organisation's resources are of fundamental importance for any form of strategic planning, whether positioning-based or resource-based. A critical awareness of the nature of the organisation's resources must be allied to the ability to improve them in ways that enhance competitiveness.

Position audit

is the part of the planning process which examines
the current state of the organisation in respect of:

1 Resources (assets and finance)

2 Products, brands and markets

3 Operating systems

4 Internal organisation

5 Current results

6 Returns to shareholders

Resource Audit

A resource audit is an internal review of all aspects of the resources the organisation uses

Some resources are easy to define, identify and measure (eg plant and machinery, finance). Others are more problematic (such as management skills, technical competence and culture.)

Typical resources (9Ms)
■ **Materials** – costs, security of supply
■ **Men and women (staff)** – skills, number, morale
■ **Management** – skills, capacity
■ **Machinery** – age, efficiency, capacity
■ **Money** – sources, gearing, cashflow
■ **Markets** – products, customers
■ **Make-up** – culture and structure, brands, patents
■ **Methods** – structure, outsourcing, JIT
■ **Management information** – ideas, innovation, information systems, performance measurement

Resources are only of value if they are properly organised: **management** and **organisation** are vital resources.

Limiting factors

'a factor which at any time or over a period may limit the activity of an entity, often one where there is a shortage or difficulty of supply'

Resources should be used **efficiently**; this requires:

- **Effectiveness** – how well they are used
- **Economy** – containment of cost

The value chain can be used to help identify the activities which create value for an organisation's customers.

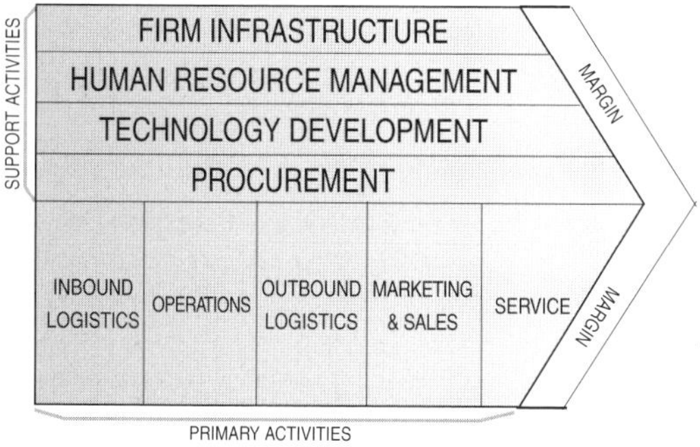

A firm's value chain is connected to what Porter calls a **value system.**

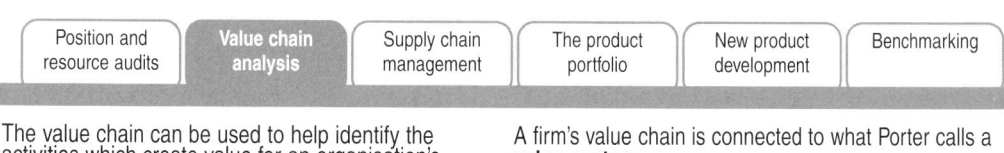

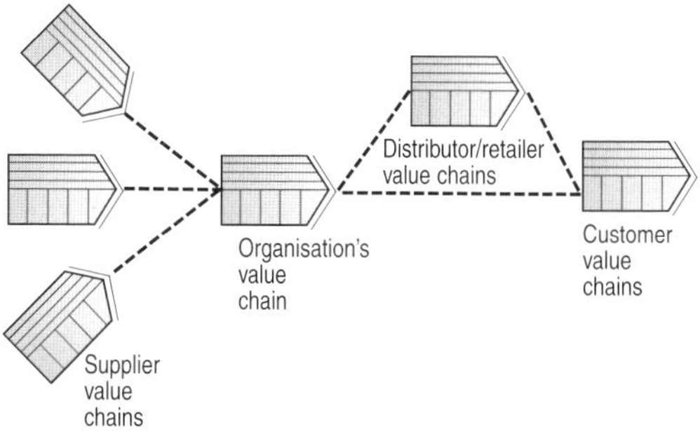

Note: The value chain was designed for use in a manufacturing context, and can be difficult to apply to service organisations. *Stabell & Fjeldstad* developed an alternative model – the **value shop** – in relation to service organisations. The value shop highlights the importance of utilising expertise in order to create value for customers.

The **margin** is the excess the customer is prepared to **pay** over the **cost** to the firm of obtaining resource inputs and providing value activities. It represents the **value created** by the **value activities** themselves and by the **management of the linkages** between them. **Linkages** connect the activities in the value chain. The activities affect one another and therefore must be co-ordinated.

Using the value chain. A firm can secure competitive advantage in several ways.

- Invent new or better ways to do activities
- Combine activities in new or better ways
- Manage the linkages in its own value chain
- Manage the linkages in the value system

	Traditional costing systems	Value chain cost analysis: an alternative
Focus	Manufacturing operations	Customers Value perceptions
Cost objects	Products Functions Expense heads	Value-creating activities Product attributes
Organisational focus	Cost and responsibility centres	Strategic business units Value creating activities
Linkages	1 Largely ignored 2 Cost allocations and transfer prices reflect interdependencies	Recognised and maximised
Cost drivers	Simple volume measures	Strategic decisions
Accuracy	High apparent precision	Low precision Indicative answers

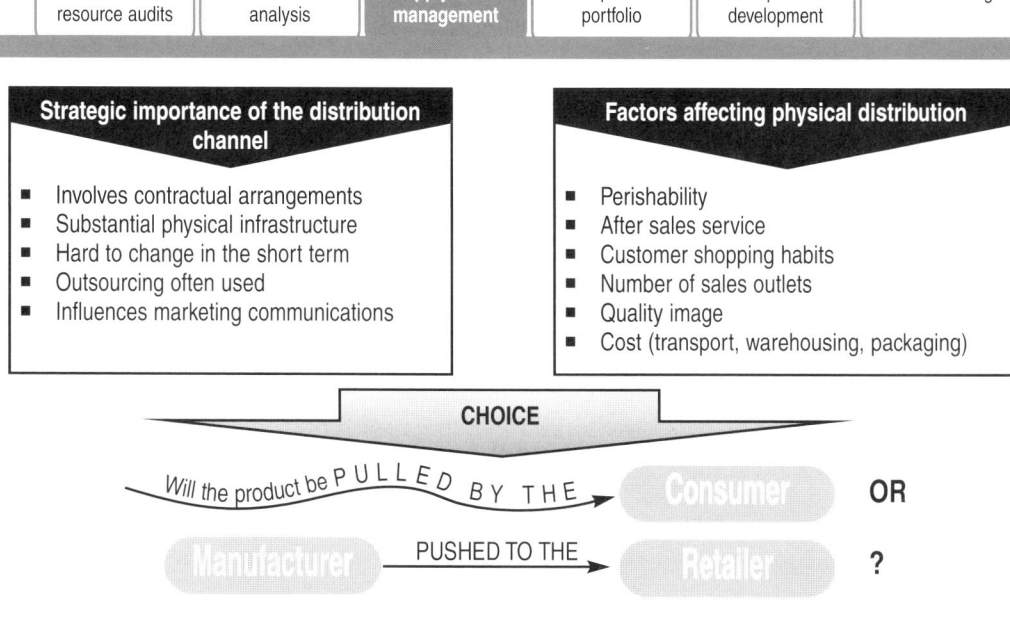

Strategic importance of the distribution channel

- Involves contractual arrangements
- Substantial physical infrastructure
- Hard to change in the short term
- Outsourcing often used
- Influences marketing communications

Factors affecting physical distribution

- Perishability
- After sales service
- Customer shopping habits
- Number of sales outlets
- Quality image
- Cost (transport, warehousing, packaging)

CHOICE

Will the product be P U L L E D B Y T H E ⟶ **Consumer** OR

Manufacturer PUSHED TO THE ⟶ **Retailer** ?

Supply chain management

A **network**, rather than a **pipeline**, of close links and greater co-operation, by which the firm aims to manage the chain from the input of resources to delivery to the customer.

Suppliers ➡

This can be achieved via

- Reduction in number of suppliers
- Reduction in number of customers
- Price and inventory co-ordination
- Linked computer systems
- Supplier involvement in product development
- Logistics design
- Joint problem solving
- Supplier representation on site

➡ **Customers**

The company's offerings to the market are fundamental to its success. They must be kept under review so that there is a suitable mix. The **product life cycle** is an important concept, and strategies must be appropriate to stage in life cycle. But product life cycle must be applied with care. We can distinguish 3 aspects of 'product'.

Product class (or **generic product**)
– a broad category

Product form
– type within the category

Brand
– The specific product

Product life cycle

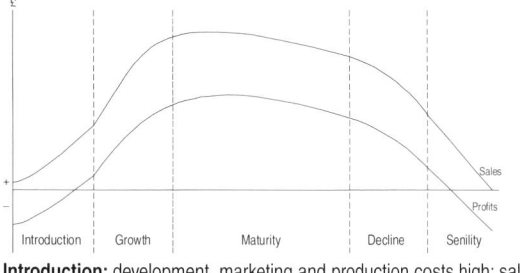

Introduction: development, marketing and production costs high; sales volume low; loss maker; negative cash flow.

Growth: sales volumes accelerate, profits rise, but cash flow likely to remain negative; competitors enter the market but overall market sales grow. High advertising costs. Additional features added to product.

Maturity: longest period; no market growth but profits good, and cash flow positive. High levels of competition so price becomes more sensitive.

Decline: product superceded; sales fall, over-capacity in industry; some players leave market. Those that remain try to find niches.

Portfolio analysis is applicable to products, market segments and SBUs. There are four basic strategies:

| **Build** Invest for market share growth | **Hold** Maintain current position | **Harvest** Manage for profit in the short term | **Divest** Release resources for use elsewhere |

The BCG Matrix

Market growth		High	Low
	High	Star	Question mark
	Low	Cash cow	Dog

Relative market share

Stars – build
Cash cows – hold or harvest
Question marks – build or harvest
Dogs – divest or hold

Problems with the BCG matrix

- Rather simplistic

- Strong brand may give competitive strength despite relatively low market share

- Ignores innovation

- Dogs and question marks may be needed to complete a range

- High market growth assumed to be attractive. But will require significant investment which may not be available.

- Ignores competitors other than market leader

- Does not indicate overall best mix or *how* to build stars and question marks.

The **development of new products** (innovation) is an important aspect of a firm's strategy. New products can **overcome entry barriers** and help give a company a **balanced portfolio**.

How are they new?

- New to the world
- New product line
- Additions to product line
- Repositioning
- Improvements/revisions
- Cost reductions

How is it approached?

- Leader strategy: high cost of R&D, potential high reward, high risk

- Follower strategy: lower cost, less R&D expertise needed, lower risk, reduced reward

The management accountant can help by analysing the cost components of the new product. This may lead to the removal of superfluous features.

New product development should be controlled by subjecting projects to a series of **gates**, (or review meetings) to decide whether they have made the required progress and to determine what must be achieved to pass the next gate.

Benchmarking involves establishing **targets** and **comparators** against which to compare performance. It provides management with a means of identifying how well areas of an organisation are performing, with a view to improving the performance of those areas which are currently underperforming.

Process for benchmarking

1 Ensure senior management commitment

2 Determine areas for study and set objectives

3 Understand process and identify key measures

4 Select organisations to benchmark

5 Measure own and others' performance

6 Compare performance and discuss results

7 Design and implement improvements

8 Monitor improvements

**The questions to ask
(Johnson, Scholes & Whittington)**

- Why are these products or services **provided at all**?

- Why are they provided **in that particular way**?

- What are the examples of **best practice** elsewhere?

- How should **activities be reshaped** in the light of the best practice comparisons?

Problems with benchmarking

Benchmarking can produce improvements in the value system but this is not guaranteed.

- It tends to improve the **efficiency** with which systems work rather than the **effectiveness** of their outputs.

- Concentrates on 'doing things right' rather than necessarily 'doing the right thing'.

- Comparison with similar systems ignores the emergence of **substitutes**.

- It is only ever a catching-up exercise rather than the development of anything new.

- It does not indicate **how** competitors may be overtaken.

- It has significant costs, not least in management time.

- It can be a threat to commercial security.

5: Generic strategies

After an organisation has analysed its current strategic position, it then has to consider its strategic options.

It is unlikely that the choice of strategy will change repeatedly from year to year. Most businesses have some sort of core business determining their direction over time. The choice of 'how to compete' is a crucial strategic decision.

There are three categories of strategic choice.

STRATEGIC CHOICE

Institutional strategies
Method of growth – acquisition or organic

Product market strategies
Where to compete
Direction of growth
Ansoff's Matrix

Competitive strategies
How to compete
Porter's generic strategies

The purpose of competitive strategy is to create a position within an industry which copes successfully with the five competitive forces and thereby yields a superior return on investment for the firm and a sustainable competitive advantage. A firm can use its value chain to help design its competitive strategy.

Cost leadership

Aim to be the **lowest cost producer** in the industry as a whole

Aspects of cost

- Economies of scale
- Use the newest production technology
- Learning curve effect
- Productivity improvement
- Minimisation of overheads
- Favourable access to inputs
- Use IT to monitor costs

Differentiation

Aim to exploit a product or service perceived as unique within the industry as a whole

Aspects of differentiation

Breakthrough products – radical performance advantage

Improved products – more cost-effective

Competitive products – unique combinations of features

- Brand image
- Special product features
- Unique combination of **value activities**

Focus

Activity is restricted to a particular **segment** of the market. Either cost leadership or differentiation strategy is then pursued. Such concentrated effort can be more effective, but the segment may be attacked by a larger firm.

Generic strategies and the five competitive forces

Competitive force	Advantages		Disadvantages	
	Cost leadership	Differentiation	Cost leadership	Differentiation
New entrants	Economies of scale raise entry barriers	Brand loyalty and perceived uniqueness are entry barriers		
Substitutes	Firm not as vulnerable to the threat of substitutes as its less cost-effective competitors	Customer loyalty is a weapon against substitutes		
Customers	Customers cannot drive down prices further than the next most efficient competitor	Customers have no comparable alternative Brand loyalty should reduce price sensitivity and prevent price wars	Very internally focused. Ignores customers' needs	Customers may no longer need the differentiating factor Sooner or later, customers become price sensitive
Suppliers	Flexibility to deal with cost increases	Higher margins can offset vulnerability to supplier price rises	Increase in input costs can reduce price advantages	
Industry rivalry	Firm remains profitable when rivals collapse through excessive price competition	Unique features reduce direct competition	Technological change will require capital investment, or make production cheaper for competitors Competitors learn via imitation Cost concerns ignore product design or marketing issues	Imitation narrows differentiation Differentiating factors may be undermined if rivals develop significantly better technology

Advantages of a focus strategy	Drawbacks of a focus strategy
■ A niche may be more secure so a firm can insulate itself from competition ■ A firm can specialise in one particular area of expertise and not spread its resources too thinly ■ Because the segment is smaller than the market as a whole, a firm will need less investment in marketing operations than if it was competing across the whole market	■ Economies of scale which could be gained by serving a wider market may be sacrificed ■ Market segment may not be large enough to secure sufficient returns to satisfy investors in the long run ■ Risk of larger competitors, with greater resources, moving into the market segment ■ Segment may become less distinct from the main market meaning it is no longer an identifiable niche

Porter argues that if a firm does not follow one of the three generic strategies it will be **stuck in the middle** and can only make low profits.

But there are problems with Porter's model (and perhaps with strategic models more generally):

- What does cost leadership actually mean? It is not necessarily the same as 'low price'.
- Does differentiation necessarily mean 'higher price'?
- How is the 'industry' defined?
- Is strategy determined at SBU or corporate level?

Importantly, many companies actually pursue 'stuck-in-the-middle' strategies quite successfully. Porter's model no longer reflects the full range of competitive strategies an organisation can choose from, and underplays the role the customer plays in defining value for money.

Strategy clock

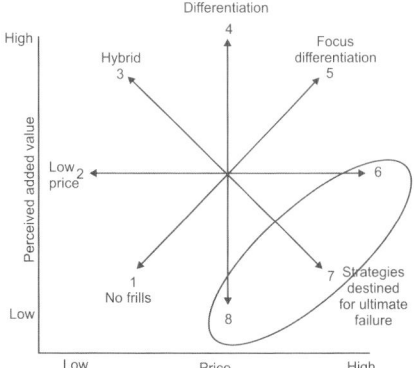

6: Directions and methods of growth

Topic List

Product-market strategies

Organic growth, mergers and acquisitions

International expansion

Joint ventures, alliances and franchising

Divestment

As well as choosing a generic strategy for how to compete, a firm has to decide the mix of products and markets it wants to target in order to achieve growth.

A firm also has to choose whether to grow organically, or through external growth.

However, although strategic choices often focus on growth and development, there may also be occasions when a firm has to divest of underperforming assets or has to rationalise costs.

Ansoff described four possible growth strategies in the **growth vector matrix**.

PRODUCT

	Existing	**New**
Existing **MARKET**	**Market penetration** ■ Maintain or increase market share ■ Dominate growth markets ■ Drive out competition from mature markets ■ Increase usage by existing customers	**Product development** ■ Launch new products ■ May require new competences ■ Forces competitors to follow suit ■ Discourages newcomers
New	**Market development** ■ New markets for current products ■ New geographic areas - export ■ New package sizes ■ New distribution channels ■ Differential pricing to suit new segments	**Diversification** Related / Unrelated (conglomerate) Vertical / Horizontal Forward Backward New **competences** will be required

Horizontal integration

Development into activities that are competitive with, or complementary to, present activities; eg, electricity companies selling gas. Offers economies of scale.

Conglomerate diversification

- Spreads risk
- May obtain synergy (eg utilising distribution channels, pooling R+D.)

However:

- Unfamiliarity with new segments increases risk
- More opportunities to go wrong
- Cultural and management integration mismatches

Vertical integration

The organisation becomes its own supplier (backward vertical integration) or its own distributor (forward vertical integration).

- Secures supplies
- Stronger relationship with end-users
- Profits from all parts of value system
- Creates barriers to entry

However:

- Increases reliance on a particular aspect of economic demand
- Does not offer significant economies of scale
- Increases ratio of fixed costs vs variable costs
- Risk of internal inefficiencies, in the absence of open market transactions in the supply chain.

6: Directions and methods of growth

We can summarise possible expansion methods by looking at whether they are internal or external, and whether they take place in a firm's home country or internationally. (*Lynch* – Expansion method matrix)

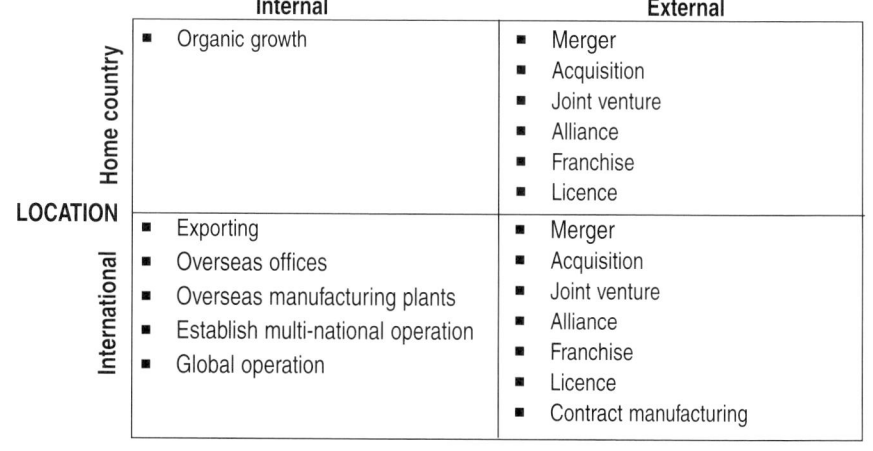

GROWTH

	Internal	**External**
Home country	■ Organic growth	■ Merger ■ Acquisition ■ Joint venture ■ Alliance ■ Franchise ■ Licence
International	■ Exporting ■ Overseas offices ■ Overseas manufacturing plants ■ Establish multi-national operation ■ Global operation	■ Merger ■ Acquisition ■ Joint venture ■ Alliance ■ Franchise ■ Licence ■ Contract manufacturing

LOCATION

Organic growth	Mergers and acquisitions
The development of internal resources	■ Provides access to a variety of resources: products; managers; suppliers; production facilities; technology and skills; distribution facilities; marketing advantages; cash; tax losses
■ Supports **learning** and is supported by it	■ Can overcome barriers to entry
■ Encourages innovation as source of growth	■ Can spread risk
■ Consistent culture and management style	■ Can defend against predators
■ Provides economies of scale	However, many acquisitions fail to enhance shareholder value.
■ Ease of control	■ Cost: the price is often too high
However:	■ Cultural problems, especially in management
■ Can be slow	■ Top management egos can warp judgement
■ Not good for dealing with barriers to entry	■ Professional advisers drive the market
■ Firm has to bear all risks internally	■ Customers may be disturbed by changes

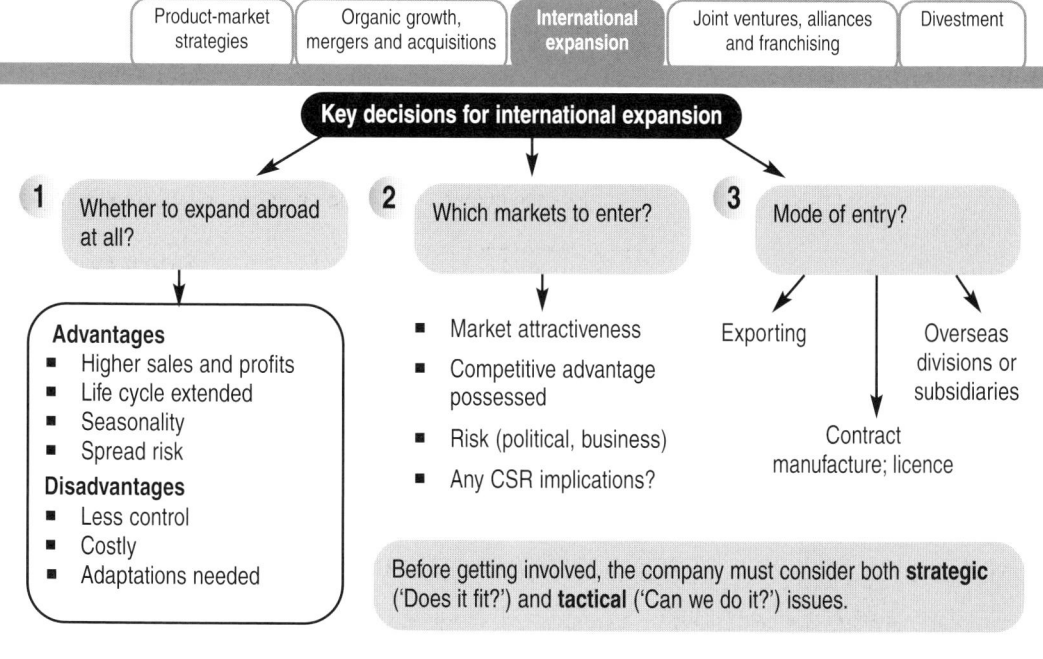

Product-market strategies | Organic growth, mergers and acquisitions | **International expansion** | Joint ventures, alliances and franchising | Divestment

Key decisions for international expansion

1 Whether to expand abroad at all?

2 Which markets to enter?

3 Mode of entry?

Advantages
- Higher sales and profits
- Life cycle extended
- Seasonality
- Spread risk

Disadvantages
- Less control
- Costly
- Adaptations needed

- Market attractiveness
- Competitive advantage possessed
- Risk (political, business)
- Any CSR implications?

Exporting

Contract manufacture; licence

Overseas divisions or subsidiaries

Before getting involved, the company must consider both **strategic** ('Does it fit?') and **tactical** ('Can we do it?') issues.

Joint ventures are arrangements between firms to pool their interests on a project. The mechanism is to create a new firm under joint control.

Alliances tend to be longer term and aim to complement technology, geography, markets and so on.

Advantages

- Coverage of a larger number of markets
- Reduced risk of government intervention
- Closer control over operations
- Local knowledge
- Spreading of risk and costs
- Learning from partners

However, there can be major conflicts of interest, and disagreements over:

- Profit sharing
- Investment levels
- Management
- Marketing strategy

Other arrangements include co-operative methods such as:

1 Licensing – the licenser provides rights, advice and know how in return for a royalty

2 Franchising – the franchiser provides expertise and brand; the franchisee provides capital and is responsible for day-to-day operations

3 Sub-contracting – enhanced access to resources, reduce overheads

6: Directions and methods of growth

On occasions, rather than looking to grow, firms may divest themselves of non-core activities or businesses in declining sectors.

Reasons for divestment

- To rationalise a business and concentrate resources on core activities (especially if current business combination is destroying value rather than creating it)
- To sell off subsidiaries at a profit
- To make a profit by buying and selling companies
- To get out while the going is good
- To raise funds to invest elsewhere

Demergers and **management buyouts** have become more common as conglomerates go out of fashion.

7: Evaluating Strategic Options

Topic List

Evaluating Strategic Options

Risk and cost behaviour

Decision techniques

In strategic investment appraisal the following approach is needed.

- *Determine what you are trying to do*
- *Assess whether the data is incomplete*
- *Recognise where estimated data is uncertain*
- *State any assumptions*

This chapter summarises how management accountants can apply decision techniques to strategic issues.

Basic tests of strategy

1 **Suitability** – relates to organisation's strategic logic; fit with circumstances?

2 **Feasibility** – can it be done/paid for?

3 **Acceptability** – will it suit different stakeholders?

Strategic uncertainties

- Trends in the industry
- Competitors' activities
- Valuing intangibles such as brands
- Evaluating marketing expenditure
- Product interrelationships

Some firms set target returns in NPV terms, using an appropriate **cost of capital**. The cost of capital may be based upon:

- The weighted average cost of capital (WACC)
- The marginal cost of capital
- The opportunity cost of capital
- Adjustments to allow for the risks of a particular project
- A return based upon the capital asset pricing model

Ultimately, investment decisions for companies are supposed to **increase shareholder value**

- Shareholder value analysis
- Economic value added

If you need to 'evaluate a strategy' in your exam, you should consider its suitability, acceptability and feasibility. **Always consider suitability first**: there is no point assessing whether a strategy is acceptable or feasible if it is not suitable for the situation in hand.

Suitability	Acceptability	Feasibility
<ul><li>Exploits strengths or competences</li><li>Rectifies weaknesses</li><li>Seizes opportunities</li><li>Helps overcome threats</li><li>Satisfies organisation's goals and objectives</li><li>Fills a gap (gap analysis)</li><li>Generates/maintains competitive advantage</li><li>Does not involve undue risk</li><li>Fits with corporate culture</li><li>Fits with existing strategies</li></ul>	Needs to be acceptable to stakeholders:<ul><li>Shareholders (shareholder wealth)</li><li>Customers</li><li>Management</li><li>Staff</li><li>Suppliers</li><li>Banks</li><li>Government/local government</li><li>Local communities</li><li>Interest/pressure groups</li></ul>	Can the strategy be implemented?<ul><li>Enough money?</li><li>Skills available?</li><li>Access to technology</li><li>Access to materials or other resources if required</li><li>Management skills to lead strategy</li><li>Sufficient time to implement</li><li>Will competitors' reactions make the strategy unworkable?</li></ul>

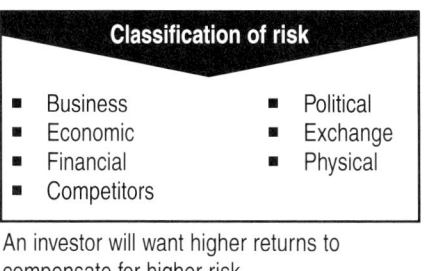

Classification of risk

- Business
- Economic
- Financial
- Competitors
- Political
- Exchange
- Physical

An investor will want higher returns to compensate for higher risk.

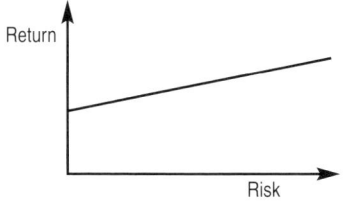

Different stakeholders have different perceptions of risk. Risk **can** be managed, however:

- A strategy which is simply too risky will not be followed
- Some risks can be dealt with by insurance or contingency plans
- An allowance for risk can be built into the target return for the project
- With a portfolio, risks can be balanced against each other

Operational gearing (the ratio of fixed to variable costs) is an important indicator of risk. Businesses with high fixed costs and low variable costs may have high **breakeven levels**.

Quantitative and non quantitative methods can be employed to help appraise strategic decisions.

Cost/benefit analysis

Especially relevant to the public sector

Ranking and scoring

Objectives are weighted according to their importance, and strategies scored according to which objectives they achieve

Decision trees

Used to arrive at expected values of mutually exclusive choices

Decision matrix

Analyses the payoff for any given action

Sensitivity analysis

Quantifies the sensitivity of a strategy to external circumstances

But remember: strategic decisions often have a long time scale and involve data which may be unreliable, so a firm cannot guarantee to always make the 'correct' decision.

Notes

8: Strategic marketing

Topic List

Marketing

Branding

Buyer behaviour

Customer relationship marketing

The customer portfolio

Databases and marketing

E-marketing

Marketing plays a key part in an organisation's strategy, and can help it fulfil its mission and objectives.

In recent years, the internet has allowed organisations to develop new marketing activities as well.

However, 'products' and 'customers' remain the two key aspects of marketing, because they are the primary sources of revenue for an organisation.

The **marketing concept** is the idea that the organisation's key task is to find out the needs, wants and values of a **target market** and to adapt the organisation to delivering them.

Marketing

is the management process which identifies, anticipates and supplies customer requirements profitably.

The organisation must commit itself to supplying what customers need. This is called a marketing orientation.

The marketing mix (4 Ps) summarises the variables that need to be considered in marketing.

The organisation must decide

- What target markets should be selected for development

- How to offer its product or service

- How to establish a marketing system and organisation

- How to develop, implement and control a marketing plan

MARKETING

- Key part of business strategy
- Can be a source of competitive advantage
- Two approaches – product-led or customer-led

PRODUCT-LED APPROACH

Products are the source of profits
- Direct product profitability (DPP)
- Brand strategies

CUSTOMER-LED APPROACH

Customers are the source of profits
- Customer profitability analysis (CPA)
- Life cycle costing (LCC)
- Customer relationship marketing (CRM)

Five steps for creating a marketing strategy:

1. Define the market
2. Determine performance differentials in terms of competitors, products and customers
3. Get to know the competitors' products and markets
4. Profile competitors' strategies
5. Determine the strategic marketing strategy

8: Strategic marketing

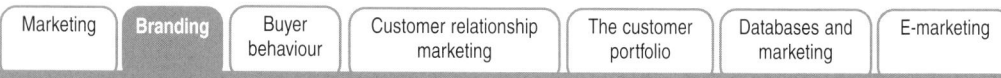

Reasons for branding

- **Product differentiation**
- **Product identification**
- Increased **acceptance** (wholesalers/retailers)
- Reduces importance of **price differentials**
- Encourage **brand loyalty**
- Strong brands form **barriers to entry**
- Brands have **longer lifecycles** than products
- Faster/less risky entry to **new markets** or introduction of **new products**
- Simplified analysis of costs/revenues
- Facilitate **self-selection** and easier for manufacture to obtain optimum **display space** in shops

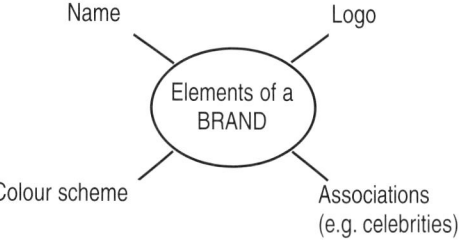

Branding strategies

- Line extension
- Brand extensions
- Multi-branding
- New brands
- Co-branding

Marketing managers need to assess **why** buyers purchase their goods or services, to help determine the marketing strategy used for different goods or services:

- Physiological needs
- Safety needs
- Social needs
- Status/ego needs
- Self-fulfilment needs.

Market segmentation

Market segmentation recognises that every market consists of potential buyers with different needs and different buying behaviour. This could be particularly relevant for an organisation following a **focus strategy**.

Key implications of market segmentation:

- Identifies groups of people (or organisations) with common needs and preferences who might therefore react to 'market stimuli' in much the same way.

- Each market segment can become a target market for an organisation, and will require its own unique marketing mix if the organisation is to exploit it successfully.

8: Strategic marketing

Markets will also be affected by the range of different buyers in them:

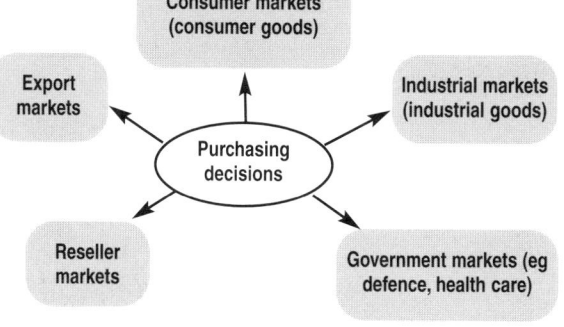

Industrial markets

- Demand for industrial goods is derived from the consumer goods they are used to produce.

- Industrial buyers (B2B markets) are more rational in their decision-making than are many consumers. They are motivated by:

    - Quality and reliability
    - Price
    - Delivery date
    - Credit terms
    - After-sales service
    - Purchasing procedures

Customers vary significantly

Frequency and volume of purchases
Reasons for buying
Sensitivity to price changes
Reaction to sales promotions
Overall attitude to company/product

Customer retention

Will they come back for more? Front line staff are *vital*.

Repeat buyers

- Don't need to be persuaded
- Don't need special deals
- Need less sales staff
- Account already set up

Key account management

Concentrate effort on the most valuable customers

Relationship management

Relationship management enhances satisfaction by meeting *individual* customer needs

- Build customer database
- Customer-oriented service systems
- Extra direct customer contact

Transactional marketing	Relationship marketing
Importance of single sale	Importance of customer relations
Importance of product features	Importance of customer benefits
Short time scale	Longer time scale
Less emphasis on service	High customer service
Quality is concern of production	Quality is concern of all
Competitive commitment	High customer commitment
Persuasive communication	Regular communication

The need for customer relationship management

- Customers can easily switch suppliers (particularly with internet price and product comparison sites)
- Retaining customers is cheaper than attracting new ones
- Need to retain customers to be able to widen product range
- Hard to attract new customers to mature markets

Customer relationship management strategies

- Customer focused staff incentive schemes
- Consistent standards
- Obtain detailed customer information
- Monitor relationships and understand customer behaviour
- Encourage loyalty (eg reward cards)

Six markets model (Payne)

- Relationship marketing extends beyond the customer
- Superior customer value can only be delivered if there are suitable relationships in all six markets

1. Customer markets
2. Referral markets
3. Supplier markets
4. Recruitment markets
5. Influence markets
6. Internal markets

Tools for analysing the customer portfolio

① Marketing audit

To establish:

- Size of customer base
- Order sizes
- Product profitability
- Market segment profitability
- Market share
- Growth and prospects
- Demand
- Competition/substitutes

② Key customer analysis

- Who are the key customers?
- What is the relationship of customer to product?
- How important are they in relation to total market?
- Attitudes and behaviour of customer
- Financial performance
- Profitability of their orders

③ Customer profitability analysis

This varies from customer to customer because of customer specific costs such as discounts, distribution costs, complexity of orders and credit given.

- Use it to identify your most profitable/ most expensive customers
- But remember customers often buy a range of products not a single product
- And remember customer profitability may change over customer lifecycle

The customer lifecycle

- Promotional expense is front-loaded; sales grow with time
- Consumer incomes rise with time; early purchases are likely to be basic – may be more differentiated later

Database marketing

> is the analysis and use of customer databases to aid in the direct marketing of products and services

Offers significant benefits to a business:

- Identify the best customers (recency of last purchase, frequency of purchase, monetary value of purchases)

- Tailor e-marketing messages based on customer usage, so can target customers more effectively

- Cross-sell related and complementary products.

Data warehouses provide a single point for storing a coherent, non-volatile set of information which can be used across an organisation for management analysis and decision-making.

Data warehouses improve data quality by reducing the risk of different people using different data during a decision-making process. They also improve the speed of responses to business queries.

Data warehouses are primarily used for storing data rather than analysing data. By contrast, **data mining** is primarily concerned with analysing data and identifying patterns and relationships in that data.

A **data warehouse** consists of a database, containing data from various operational systems, and reporting and query tools.

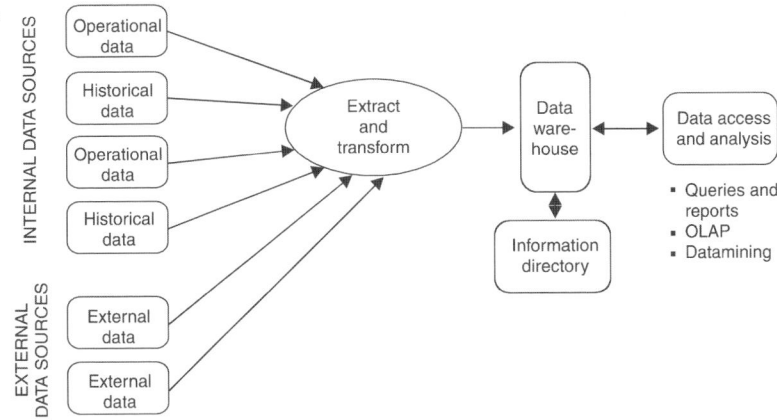

Data mining software looks for hidden patterns and relationships in large pools of data, using statistical analysis tools and intelligence techniques. Data mining can give organisations a better insight into customer behaviours.

8: Strategic marketing

E-marketing has been defined as 'the application of the Internet and related digital technologies to achieve marketing objectives' (Chaffey).

Functions of Internet marketing	**Specific benefits of Internet marketing**
■ Creating company and product awareness	■ Global reach
■ Branding via website advertising	■ Lower cost
■ Offering incentives	■ Ability to track and measure results
■ Lead generation via interaction	■ 24 hour marketing
■ Customer service	■ Personalisation/'one to one'
■ Email databases	■ More interesting campaigns
■ Driving online transactions	■ Better conversion rate

Any online e-communication must be consistent with the overall marketing goals and current marketing efforts of the organisation.

E-marketing planning

Competitor analysis	Scan competitor websites; benchmark e-commerce services
Intermediary analysis	Search portals for new approaches; research competitor intermediary policy; identify and compare intermediaries.
Marketing audit	Measurement: acquisition costs, leads, sales, ROI. Use web analytics to measure impact of leads; sales and brand effects delivered over the Internet; create online CRM capability.
Objective setting	Online revenue contribution
Strategy	Online value proposition; identify target online segments
Tactics	Use Internet to vary the extended product
	Consider new channel structures
	Automate processes: auto-responder, FAQs, virtual assistants
	Online branding
	Online marketing communications, eg email selling, search engine advertising

Characteristics of the media of e-marketing – the 6 Is

Plans should accommodate and exploit the 6 'I' characteristics

Independence of location	Global reach of electronic products and services opens previously inaccessible markets for exploitation
Industry structure	Redesign of business processes; new market boundaries and segments; IT-enabled services
Integration	Widespread, effective use of detailed customer information throughout business enables value added through product configuration, pricing, delivery and so on.
Interactivity	Customers can participate in a marketing dialogue; communications and responses can be specifically targeted.
Individualisation	Tailored products, services and communications
Intelligence	Detailed customer information can be collected *via* interactivity

E-marketing and the marketing mix (7Ps)

1. **Product**   interactivity, more information, opportunities to customise and augment the product

2. **Price**   the Internet has made pricing very competitive; increased price transparency and the ability to 'shop around'

3. **Place**   new market places and channel structures. Since the Internet has global reach, customer convenience is very important.

4. **Promotion**   reach more customers; target more specifically; use of email; banner advertising

5. **People**   people can be replaced with automated processes, such as 'FAQ' pages on web

6. **Process**   new processes are required for online marketing, linking to other operational systems

7. **Physical evidence**   customers' experience such as ease of use of website, navigation, availability and overall performance. Responsiveness to email enquiries is a key aspect.

                     Might also include user generated content (eg product reviews), or samples (eg extracts from books on Amazon).

9: Information systems and strategy

This chapter examines the aspects of information management that have strategic significance. Strategic information is used to plan the objectives of the organisation, and to assess whether the objectives are being met in practice.

Information systems and information technology are playing an increasingly dynamic role in contemporary organisations, while the internet is also opening up new business opportunities and ways of interacting with existing and potential customers.

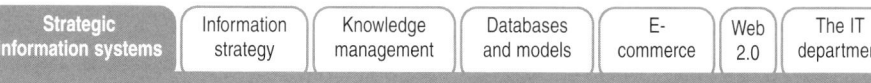

Strategic information is used to plan the objectives of the organisation and to assess whether those objectives are being met in practice.

Strategic information is:

- Derived from internal and external sources
- Summarised at a high level
- Relevant to the long term
- Concerned with the whole organisation
- Both quantitative and qualitative
- Uncertain

The Anthony hierarchy

Types of strategic information system

- **Executive information system** (EIS) helps senior managers take strategic decisions.

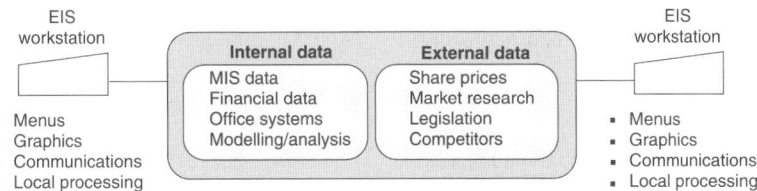

- **Management information system** (MIS) provides operational reports on existing operations.

- **Decision Support System** (DSS) has high levels of analytical power and aids decisions on issues subject to high levels of uncertainty.

- **Value added networks** facilitate the adding of value to products by the strategic use of information. They can link organisations and may be businesses in their own right. Examples are airline booking systems and EDI systems between suppliers and manufacturers.

9: Information systems and strategy

The **information systems (IS) strategy** is the long-term plan for systems to exploit information in order to support business strategies or create new strategic options.

The **information technology (IT) strategy** is concerned with selecting, operating and managing the technological element (the hardware and the software) necessary to implement the IS strategy.

The **information management (IM) strategy** deals with the roles of the people involved in the use of IT assets, the relationships between them and design of the management processes needed to exploit IT and to control it.

Strategic information systems are systems at any level of an organisation that change goals, processes, products, services or environmental relationships with the aim of gaining competitive advantage.

A strategic approach is needed because IS/IT:

- Involve high costs
- Are critical to the success of many organisations
- Are now used as part of the commercial strategy in the battle for competitive advantage
- Have an impact on customer service
- Affect all levels of management and staff
- May lead to structural changes in an organisation
- Affect the way management information is created and presented
- Require effective management to obtain the maximum benefit
- Involve many stakeholders inside and outside the organisation

IT and corporate strategy

Porter and Millar (P & M)

- IT transforms the **value chain** and the **product**
- Products have increasingly large **information content**.
- IT changes industry structure *via* the **five forces**
- IT enhances competitive advantage by **reducing costs** and making **differentiation** easier.

Competing in the information age (P&M)

1. Assess **information intensity** in products and processes.
2. Determine the **role of IT** in the industry structure.
3. Identify the ways IT can create **competitive advantage**.
4. Identify how IT might create **new business**.
5. Develop a **plan** to exploit it.

Developing the IT strategy (Earl)

Continuing development of the IT strategy requires:

- Constant reference to the overall business strategy
- Attention to compatibility of technologies
- Consideration of wider implications
- Proper planning of significant charges, perhaps using SSADM

Three leg analysis (Earl)

- **Business led**, starting with overall objectives
- **Infrastructure led**, starting with business-critical transaction processing systems
- **Mixed**, organisation encourages ideas to exploit existing IS and IT resources.

Critical success factors (CSFs) can help to determine the information requirements of an organisation: they are the key operational goals.

Managers should focus on a small number of objectives, and information systems should focus on providing information to enable managers to monitor these.

Rockart identifies four sources of CSFs.

- The industry
- The company itself
- The environment
- Temporal organisational factors

Information audit aims to establish the information needs of users and how they can be met.

1 **Information needs assessment**, usually through interviews and questionnaires.

2 **Information analysis** examines the information provided by the current system.

3 **Gap analysis** compares needs from stage 1 with what is provided (stage 2)

Earl's grid analyses current IS use.

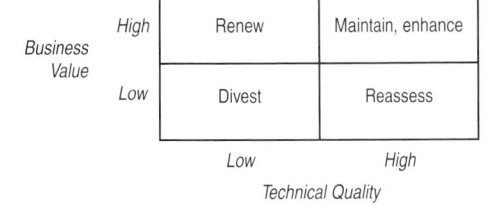

Technical Quality

Strategic grid

McFarlan and McKenney devised a matrix to show four levels of dependence on IS/IT in an organisation.

Applications portfolio

Peppard developed the strategic grid into the **applications portfolio** to show the potential impact of current individual applications.

*Strategic importance of **planned** information systems*	High	Turnaround	Strategic
	Low	Support	Factory
		Low	High

*Strategic importance of **current** information systems*

*Strategic importance of individual applications in the predicted **future** competitive environment*	High	High potential	Strategic
	Low	Support	Key operational
		Low	High

*Strategic importance of individual applications in the **current** competitive environment*

The progression from data to knowledge

	Data	Information	Knowledge
Nature	Facts	Relationships between processed facts	Patterns discerned in information
Importance of context	Total	Some	Context independent
Importance to business	Mundane	Probably useful for management	May be strategically useful
Relevant IT systems	Office automation Data warehouse	Groupware Expert systems Report writing software Intranet	Data mining Intranet Expert systems

The aim of knowledge management is to **capture**, **organise** and make widely **available** all the knowledge that the organisation possesses. However, successful knowledge management requires a **culture** of knowledge sharing to be developed, not just an IT infrastructure which allows knowledge to be shared.

A database

is a collection of data organised to service many applications. The database provides convenient access to data for a wide variety of users and user needs.

A database management system (DBMS)

is the software that centralises data and manages access to the database. It is a system which allows numerous applications to extract the data they need without the need for separate files.

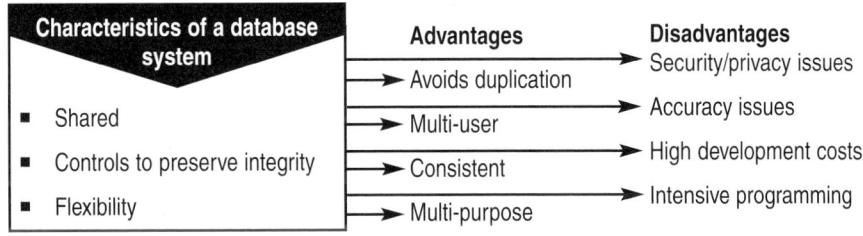

Characteristics of a database system	Advantages	Disadvantages
■ Shared	Avoids duplication	Security/privacy issues
■ Controls to preserve integrity	Multi-user	Accuracy issues
■ Flexibility	Consistent	High development costs
	Multi-purpose	Intensive programming

The internet and business operations

- Challenge to **traditional business models** including new intermediaries and direct interaction with customers
- Transparency of **pricing**
- Much **information** becomes **free to view** including many publications
- Extremely **rapid communication** at much reduced cost
- Work can be done **remotely**, hence the **virtual corporation**
- The **nature of work** is changing
- **World-wide** potential markets
- Sophisticated **market segmentation** opportunities
- **Cost** and **management/specialist effort** required to set up and run an e-commerce operation
- **Knowledge** as a strategic asset

An e-commerce strategy

Suitability

- E-commerce may constitute the whole strategy: suitability depends on matching Internet opportunities to business strengths.
- E-commerce as an extension of existing operations must be consistent with existing sales and marketing effort.

Acceptability

The main concern is likely to be the effect on any established distributors

Feasibility

- Depends on cash and skilled labour
- Introducing a new strategy should involve:
  - setting of objectives
  - study of costs and benefits
  - detailed budget
  - consideration of technical requirements

Web 2.0 allows users/potential customers to create, share and evaluate content.

Features of Web 2.0

⟹ Web-based communities — Social networks, blogs, wikis, instant messaging

⟹ Knowledge sharing — Tagging, Mashups, collective intelligence

⟹ User generated content — Capture, create and share, eg Youtube

⟹ Consumer generated content — Product review sites

Applications for business

- Locate partners, collaborators, customers and suppliers

- Advertising and marketing (eg viral marketing)

- Customer feedback

- Market intelligence

- Customer-focused approach via contribution to product development

Ethical / legal implications

- Security

- Data protection

- Copyright

- Employment policies (eg on use of social networking sites during office hours)

9: Information systems and strategy

Centralise or decentralised? In-house or outsourced?

Outsourcing IT services

- **Timeshare** of external system reduces cost, retains managerial responsibility.

- **Service** buy in (eg payroll) increases efficiency, reduces managerial effort.

- **Facility management** is long-term strategic approach to improve service and access expertise.

What to outsource?

- Functions with **limited interfaces** (eg payroll)

- Do **not** outsource **core competences** or strategically vital functions.

Service level agreement

- **Service level**: information/assistance response time; downtime limit; task deadlines; penalties if service levels not met

- **Exit route** (eg move to another supplier, back in-house)

- **Contract duration**

- **Employment issues**: migration of staff

- **Software issues**: ownership, licensing, security

- **Dependencies**: dealing with related services

Outsourcing IT services

Advantages	Disadvantages
■ Establishes costs with some certainty	■ May prevent development of strategic capability
■ Encourages planning	■ Loss of confidentiality
■ Exploits contractor's economies of scale	■ Risk of lock-in to unsatisfactory contract
■ Provides greater skill and knowledge than a small in-house operation	■ Loss of awareness and appreciation of capabilities, limitations, costs and benefits of IT
■ Resources easily scaled up or down according to demand	

9: Information systems and strategy

Notes

10: Issues in strategic management

Topic List

Managing projects

Lean systems

Re-engineering and innovation

Organisation structure

This chapter brings together certain discrete issues that require strategic management attention, and are major business management activities.

Major projects have a strategic impact and require strategic management input. PRINCE 2 is a widely used project management system: we use it here to illustrate the strategic dimension.

Management

PRINCE 2 recognises four layers of management responsibility, starting at the strategic apex and possibly involving an executive committee to translate strategies into projects.

Business case

A PRINCE 2 project is driven by its business case: this is a reasoned account of what is to be achieved and why it is important. These concepts apply equally to the public and not-for-profit sectors.

Control

The project board restricts authorisation to one project stage at a time and manages by exception.

Processes

The eight PRINCE 2 processes are approximately equivalent to stages of the project life cycle. Several require **strategic management input**.

Directing a project continues throughout the life of a project but is restricted to higher aspects of control and decision-making.

Setting up a project deals with early fundamentals such as establishing project aims and appointment of the project board and project manager.

Controlling a stage includes a structure of reports and meetings designed to control progress against stated targets.

Closing a project includes procedures to ensure that objectives have been satisfactorily achieved and accepted.

The objective of project management is to deliver a successful project. A project is successful if it is completed at the **specified level of quality**, **on time** and **within budget**.

Process involved in project management

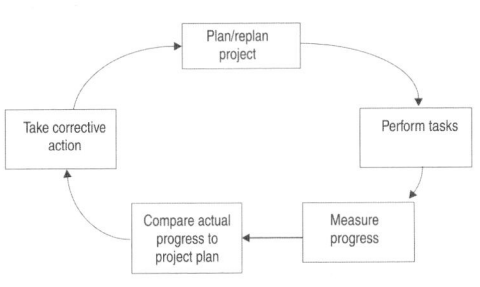

Management challenges presented by projects

- **Teambuilding** – team must 'gel' quickly and communicate effectively with each other
- **Expected problems** – avoid by planning and careful design
- **Unexpected problems** – mechanisms to resolve quickly
- **Delayed benefit** – no benefit until project over
- **Specialists** – contributions of specialists are of different importance at each stage
- **Potential for conflict** – projects involve people with different interests, which may conflict

Businesses must respond to intensified competition by **IMPROVING EFFICIENCY** and **REDUCING COSTS**, eg

- Reduced set-up times
- Reduced inventories
- Manufacturing flexibility

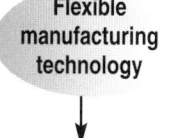

Flexible manufacturing technology

↓

- Highly automated
- Small batches
- Fast response

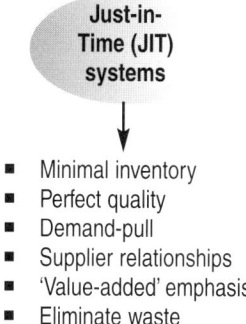

Just-in-Time (JIT) systems

↓

- Minimal inventory
- Perfect quality
- Demand-pull
- Supplier relationships
- 'Value-added' emphasis
- Eliminate waste

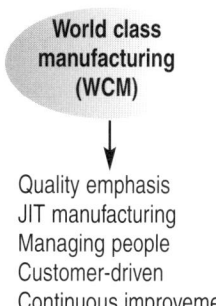

World class manufacturing (WCM)

↓

- Quality emphasis
- JIT manufacturing
- Managing people
- Customer-driven
- Continuous improvement

Lean production focuses on identifying and eliminating all non-value adding activities.

Systematic elimination of waste, with seven 'wastes' to be eliminated:

- Over-production and early production
- Waiting
- Transportation
- Inventory
- Motion
- Over-processing
- Defective units

Tools to implement lean production systems

- Just-in-time (JIT)
- Kaizen (continuous improvement)
- 5 S
- Six Sigma:
  - **D**efine customer requirements

    Measure existing performance and compare to customer requirements

    Analyse existing process

    Improve process design

    Control results and maintain new performance levels

The changes that may be made to processes may be classified as:

1   **Business automation:** the use of computerised working methods to speed up performance of tasks

2   **Business rationalisation:** the streamlining of operating procedures to eliminate obvious inefficiencies

3   **Business process re-engineering:** the **fundamental** re-thinking and **radical** re-design of business **processes** to achieve **dramatic** improvements in performance measures such as cost, quality, service and speed

(*Hammer and Champy*)

Five step approach to BPR

1 Develop the business vision and process objectives

2 Identify the processes to be redesigned

3 Understand and measure the existing processes

4 Identify change levers

5 Design and build a prototype of the new process

Problems with BPR

- May be seen simply as a cost-cutting exercise (eg reducing staff numbers)
- Ignores impact of changes on staff.
- Improves efficiency but may ignore effectiveness.

Process innovation (PI)

2 main differences to BPR:

1 Greater focus on creating **new** processes rather than improving existing processes

2 IT is often the **trigger for change** in PI whereas it is an enabler of change in BPR

Seven basic organisational structures:

Strategy is delivered through the organisation, so strategy and organisational structure need to support each other.

1 Functional (U form) ⟹ Departments identified by their function (what they do)

2 Multi-divisional (M form) ⟹ Business divided into autonomous regions/product businesses

3 Holding company ⟹ Extreme form of multi-divisional structure. Divisions are separate legal entities

4 Matrix ⟹ Attempts to ensure co-ordination across functional lines via dual authority.

5 Team based ⟹ Extends matrix structure by utilising cross-functional teams

6 Project based ⟹ Similar to team based expect that projects have a finite life and so do the project teams dealing with them

7 Transnational ⟹ Attempts to reconcile global scope and scale with local representatives.

Kanter – The Change Masters

Two contrasting organisational responses to problems caused by change and innovation.

1 **Segmentalist approach** is compartmentalised and cannot produce integrated response to new problems. Finds it hard to innovate.

2 **Integrative approach** tackles complete problems and innovates to solve them, changing the organisation if necessary. This requires three sets of skills:

- Power skills
- Problem management skills
- Change design and construction skills

To move from segmentalist to integrative:

- Encourage pride in firm's achievements
- Improve lateral communication
- Widen distribution of information about plans
- Devolve, decentralise, delayer
- Increase opportunities for innovation

The third wave

Advances in IS are seen as creating a 'third wave' of economic development comparable to the development of agriculture and industrialisation.

Specific developments:

Mass customisation of products via the Web and relationship marketing.

Disintermediation by delayering and e-commerce.

Growth of **network organisations**.

Network economies arising from the number of devices in use are becoming more important than economies of scale which depend on volume of production.

Increasing leverage of **knowledge** and rise of knowledge workers.

The new organisation and the management accountant

Delayering, empowerment, team working and flexible employment patterns will require the provision of more and different information to more and different people. Activity-based management of costs will increase as use of cross-functional responsibility centres increases.

Flexible patterns of employment will increase the need for control over temporary staff and teleworkers, and will need new ways of measuring performance.

11: Organisational change

The business environment is constantly changing and so business strategies often have to change in response to this. However, triggers for change may also come from within an organisation itself.

The change process will have to be carefully managed to ensure it is successful. Some stakeholders may support change while others will resist it. To implement changes successfully, an organisation will need to overcome resistance to change.

Change management is likely to be an important part of strategy implementation.

Change management consists of the set of activities which help people move from the present way of working to new, improved ways of working.

The change process

Change flow chart

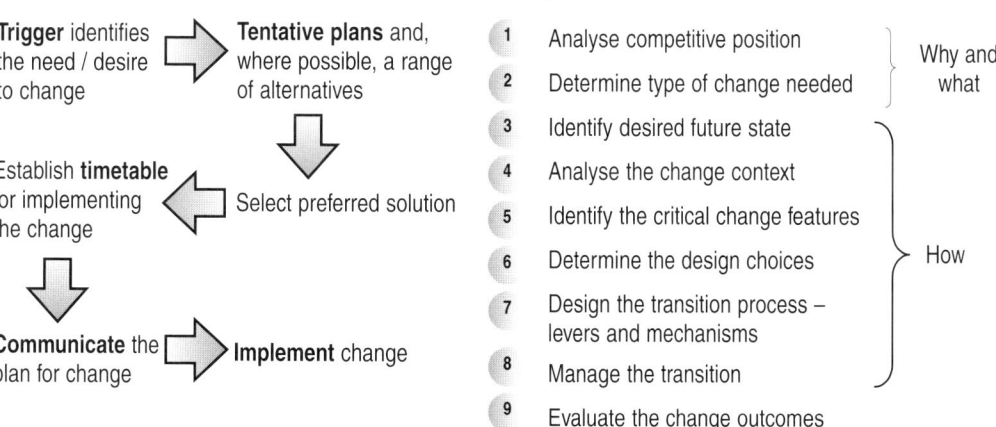

Trigger identifies the need / desire to change ⟹ **Tentative plans** and, where possible, a range of alternatives

Establish **timetable** for implementing the change ⟸ Select preferred solution

Communicate the ⟹ **Implement** change
plan for change

1 Analyse competitive position
2 Determine type of change needed
} Why and what

3 Identify desired future state
4 Analyse the change context
5 Identify the critical change features
6 Determine the design choices
7 Design the transition process – levers and mechanisms
8 Manage the transition
} How

9 Evaluate the change outcomes

An organisation may have to make a strategic change for lots of different reasons.

Environmental factors

- Level / intensity of competition
- Domestic or international economic conditions
- Government legislation
- Customer expectations / tastes
- Technology (product or process)
- Communications media and e-business
- Supply chains or distribution networks
- Globalisation
- Concern for natural environment
- Workplace structure
- Social / demographic changes

Rationalisation and cost-cutting

Concerns about market conditions and competitiveness may force organisations to downsize, rationalise or cut costs.

Mergers and acquisitions

Visible changes to name and signage, but also deeper changes to an organisation:

- Culture
- Structure
- Job roles
- Staff numbers
- Management systems
- Integration issues

External factors can be opportunities for change, not just threats.

Internally generated change is likely to be managed more proactively, effectively and efficiently than externally generated change, due to clear ownership, prior knowledge/understanding of the change, and the ability to control the nature and timing of the change.

Internal factors

- Changes in goals / activities of organisation, such as new product lines
- New organisation structure
- New senior managers; change in leadership
- Questioning authority / accepted ways
- Influence of entrepreneurs or innovators
- Acquisition of new knowledge / skills
- Poor performance

Internal triggers can cause reorganisation and restructure:

- Efficiency/effectiveness
- Centralisation/decentralisation
- Flattening of organisational hierarchy

Operational change

Organisations also have to manage change at technical and operational levels.

- Business Process Re-engineering (BPR)
- Continuous improvement culture
- Total Quality Management (TQM)

Change may also accompany organisational growth. *Greiner* suggested growing companies tend to have long periods of **evolution** (in which organisational practices remain relatively constant) interspersed by periods of **revolution** (in which there is substantial turmoil and change).

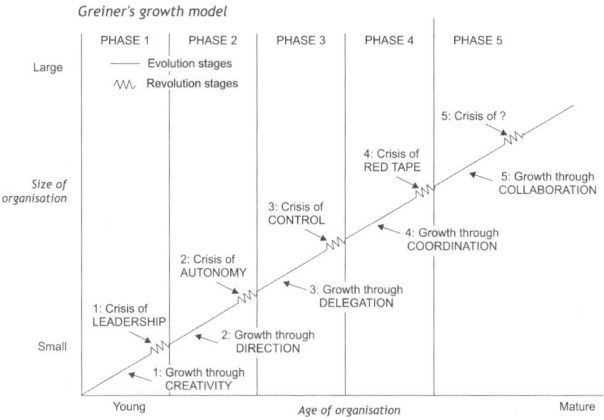

Greiner's growth model

Links between triggers: triggers do not exist in isolation

Leavitt's organisational system:

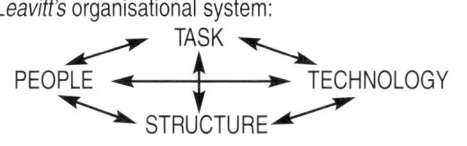

Whatever the trigger for change, managers must consider the impact on the change on the four inter-related variables and therefore the organisation as a whole.

Burke and Litwin: 12 variables to analyse the factors of organisational change

1. Mission and strategy
2. Structure
3. Task requirements and individual skills / abilities
4. External environment
5. Leadership
6. Management practices

7. Working environment
8. Motivation
9. Individual and organisational performance
10. Organisational culture
11. Systems (policies and procedures)
12. Individual needs / values

Regardless of the type of change, it is important to clearly identify the problem or the reason for change before undertaking a change programme.

Lewin's 3 stage "ice cube" model

UNFREEZE		CHANGE		REFREEZE

- Remove individuals from accustomed routines
- Consult team members
- Confront perceptions / emotions
- Positive re-inforcement

- Learn new concepts
- Encourage staff participation / involvement
- Identification with new role models
- Internalisation of new behaviours

- Embed new behaviours
- Establish new standards
- Habituation effects
- Positive reinforcement (eg rewards/bonus scheme)

Problems with the three stage model:

1. Assumes change is a structured process rather than a continuous or multi-directional process.

2. Danger that managers may interpret it as 'plan ⟶ implement ⟶ review'

3. Underplays the fundamental issue that people will only change if they feel and appreciate the need to do so

11: Organisational change

| The change process | Triggers for change | Stage models of change | **Other models of change** | Force field analysis | Resistance to change |

Gemini 4 R's Framework

Reframe	Restructuring
Create desire to change Set corporate vision	Remove elements of business that do not add value
Revitalising	**Renewal**
Find new products/markets Ensure good fit with competitive environment	Ensure people in organisation support the change and acquire necessary skills

Biological models (Morgan)

Organisation is a biological organism, constantly changing.

Two factors required to get maximum benefit from change:

1 Readiness / ability to change

2 Ability to maintain sense of continuity

Managing stability is as important as managing change.

Beer and Nohria – Theory E & Theory O

Two underlying approaches to change:

- **Theory E –** purpose of change is to increase economic value. Change is a top-down process, and the focus of change is on formal structure and systems.

- **Theory O –** purpose of change is to develop an organisation's human capability to implement strategy. Change is an emergent process, and the focus of change is on culture and cultural adjustment.

In practice, organisations need to combine elements of both Theory E and Theory O. So managers need to integrate E and O in a way which resolves the inherent tension between the two.

Bullock and Batten, planned change

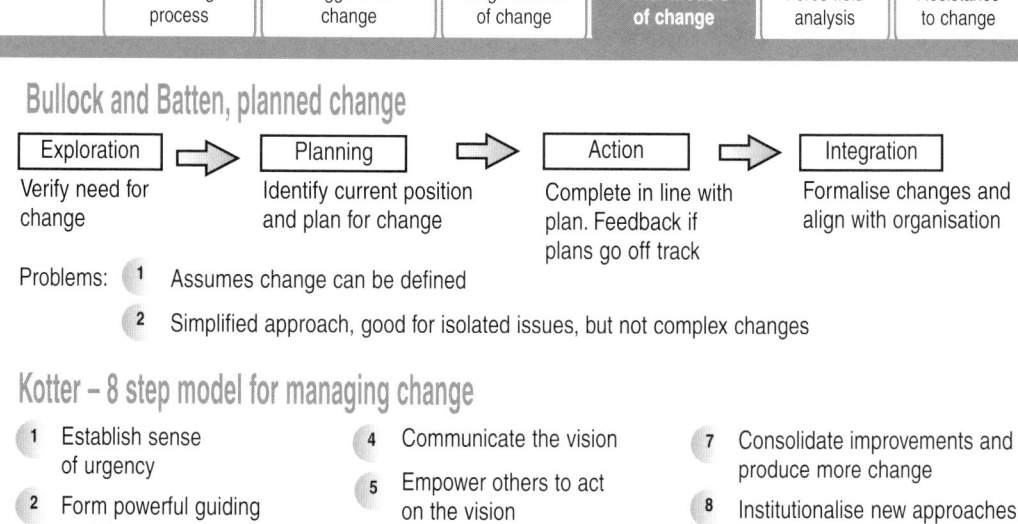

Exploration ⇒ Planning ⇒ Action ⇒ Integration

Verify need for change | Identify current position and plan for change | Complete in line with plan. Feedback if plans go off track | Formalise changes and align with organisation

Problems:
1. Assumes change can be defined
2. Simplified approach, good for isolated issues, but not complex changes

Kotter – 8 step model for managing change

1. Establish sense of urgency
2. Form powerful guiding coalition
3. Create a vision
4. Communicate the vision
5. Empower others to act on the vision
6. Plan for, and create, short term wins
7. Consolidate improvements and produce more change
8. Institutionalise new approaches

Force field analysis: identifying the factors that promote or hinder change.

For change to be successfully implemented:

- Exploit promoting forces
- Reduce hindering forces

} so that driving forces outweigh resisting forces

The status quo

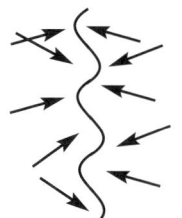

Forces driving change

- Improving quality
- Improving efficiency
- Potential savings
- Legislation/legal requirements

Forces holding back change

- Individual concerns, eg:
    - fear of the unknown
    - dislike of uncertainty
    - potential loss of power
    - potential loss of rewards
    - potential lack or loss of skills
- Cost/budget constraints
- Existing system sufficient

Forcefield analysis **doesn't give any detail about how to manage change**, or how to overcome the resistance to change. Also it presumes that all change is desirable. But on some occasions change should be resisted (if it is undesirable for the organisation's competitive advantage.)

People resist change due to to fear of the unknown:

- Confronts apathy / forces people out of comfort zones
- Reduces stability
- Do not trust change leaders or their motives for change
- Can result in restructure (job changes / losses)
- May present technological challenges

Kotter and Schlesinger's six approaches to resistance:

1. Education and communication
2. Participation and involvement
3. Facilitation and support
4. Negotiation and agreement
5. Manipulation and co-optation
6. Coercion, implicit and explicit

Relative high degree of collaboration expected from staff.

Relatively high degree of conflict expected from staff.

Underlying theme: **communication** is critical in overcoming resistance to change.

12: Implementing change

The dynamics of the external environment mean that organisations' strategies will inevitably change and evolve.

The key questions for an organisation is how rapid and extensive that change will be, and how the organisation manages the change process. Leadership is important in the change process – leaders need to have the vision to identify changes and then deliver them.

Organisations need to analyse the nature of change in order to identify the most appropriate way of managing the change.

Two key issues:

- **Extent** of change required
- **Speed** with which change needs to be introduced

Balogun and Hope Hailey

Scope of change

		Realignment	Transformation
Nature of change	**Incremental**	Adaptation	Evolution
	'Big bang'	Reconstruction	Revolution

Johnson, Scholes and Whittington

Nature of change

		Incremental	Transformational
Management role	**Proactive**	Tuning	Planned
	Reactive	Adaptation	Forced

Hard/soft changes

Hard ⟹ mechanistic. Suitable where difficulties are easily identified.

Soft ⟹ people based. Suitable when harder to define the problem.

Balogun and Hope Hailey: the change kaleidoscope

8 aspects of context:

1. Power to effect change
2. Time available
3. Scope
4. Readiness for change
5. Capability to manage change
6. Capacity for change
7. Diversity of experience
8. Preservation of organisational characteristics

6 design choices

1. Path
2. Startpoint
3. Style
4. Target
5. Roles
6. Interventions

Continuous/discontinuous change

Continuous:
- Small scale, incremental changes
- Doesn't alter paradigm or underlying strategy
- Minimises resistance

Discontinuous:
- Radical change in firms environment / operations
- Can either be a sudden one-off change, or the result of a series of incremental changes
- Very significant in the 'unfreeze' process

Top down and bottom up change

	Features	Advantages	Disadvantages
Top down	■ Determined / implemented by senior management ■ May need to be imposed	■ Fast to implement ■ Clarity of objectives	■ Unlikely to encourage ownership or commitment to the planned changes
Bottom up	■ Responsibility for change not solely with senior management ■ Consultation with staff ■ Employees contribute ideas	■ Employees have a sense of ownership of the change programme	■ Slow to implement ■ Unpredictable consequences ■ Reduced senior management control

Balogun and Hope Bailey: the cultural web

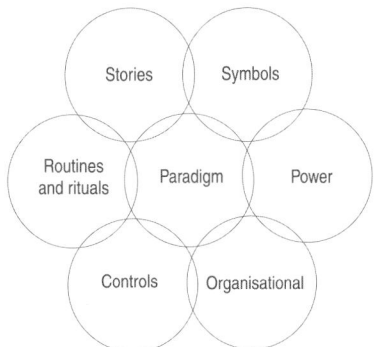

Shows cultural aspects to be considered when managing change.

McKinsey 7 'S' model

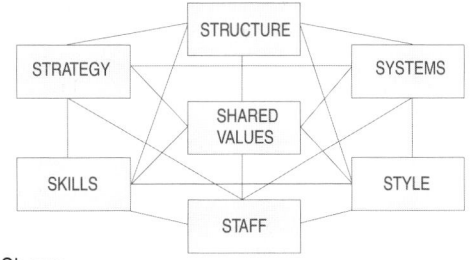

Shows:

- Link between organisation's behaviour and behaviour of individuals

- Change affects both organisations as a whole and individual people and functions within it

Cultural incompatibility is a key reason where mergers/acquisitions fail. Existing cultures should be considered at the start of the deal.

12: Implementing change

Resistance to change can occur if reasons / triggers for changes are not communicated properly:

- Appropriate method
- Appropriate timing
- Feedback opportunities provided
- Redundancy programmes handled with care

Change phase	Communication purpose
Unfreeze	Create readiness for, and understanding of, the need for change
Move	Explain changes, reduce uncertainty of impact of change, and enable staff to change
Refreeze	Keep staff informed of progress

Johnson, Scholes and Whittington identify five styles for managing change.

1. Education and communication
2. Collaboration / participation
3. Intervention
4. Direction
5. Coercion/edict

Common factors that contribute to the success of change management programmes:

- Effective support from senior management

- Buy-in from front line managers and employees

- Continuous and targeted communication

- Experienced and credible change management team

- Well-planned, well-organised approach

To buy-in to the change, employees need to hear about the change from two people:

(i) The most senior person involved in the change

(ii) Their own line manager

Why does change fail?

- Not enough sense of urgency

- Failure to create powerful support base

- Vision not clearly developed

- Vision poorly communicated

- Obstacles block the vision

- Failure to create short-term wins

- Systems, policies and skills not aligned

- Failure to anchor changes in corporate culture

- Lack of change management / implementation skills or expertise

Transactional leadership: Initiate structure and support to accomplish tasks. Focuses on systems/controls. Seek improvement rather than change.

Transformational leadership: Charisma, inspirational, intellectual motivation. This is the most appropriate approach in times of change.

Five approaches to strategic leadership

Approach	Responsibilities	
	Leader	Other managers
Strategy	Focus on strategic analysis and forming strategy	Routine operations and change management
Human assets	Development of organisation's people	Strategic management
Expertise	Technical expertise as a source of competitive advantage. Build expertise though systems and procedures.	Their own areas of expertise.
Control	Set procedures/control measures and monitor performance	Set procedures; monitor performance. Change management based on careful control
Change	Communication and motivation	Act as change agents

Control approach is a form of transactional leadership. The other four are examples of transformational leadership.

Change agent

'an individual or group that helps to bring about strategic change in an organisation.'

Role might include

- Defining the change problem
- Examining causes of the problem and considering how this can be overcome
- Suggesting possible solutions
- Selecting and implementing a solution
- Communicating information about the change throughout the organisation

Skills for a change agent:

- Encourage participation among those affected by change
- Reduce uncertainty; encourage positive action
- See the strategic picture
- Understand the relevant processes
- Think creatively, but avoid getting bogged down in detail
- Can exploit triggers for change
- Communication – across all levels of staff in the organisation
- Networking skills
- Negotiating skills (with key stakeholders) and awareness of organisational politics
- Sensitivity – in dealing with different stakeholders
- Financial analysis skills – to assess financial impacts of proposed changes

Whetten and Cameron:
Five key steps for a leader to encourage those involved to be positive about the change:

1. Establish climate of positivity
2. Create 'readiness' for change
3. Articulate a vision
4. Generate commitment to the vision
5. Institutionalising the change

Leadership skills in managing change

- Building vision
- Goal setting
- Communicating vision
- Building coalitions
- Networking
- Monitoring and controlling
- Coaching and supporting
- Negotiating
- Facilitating
- Dealing with conflict

The key role of change management in strategy implementation can be illustrated by looking at the key elements of strategic management.

Strategic change is the pro-active management of change in an organisation to achieve clearly identified strategic options.

Notes

13: Strategic control

Topic List

Planning and control

Divisional performance: ROI and RI

Comparing performance

Achieving success for the shareholder

International subsidiaries

Transfer pricing

Managerial performance

Strategic management styles

Control is necessary to help ensure that once a strategy has been implemented it either delivers the intended benefits, or that corrective action is taken if results are falling short of planned targets.

Financial measures of performance are those that the management accountant is most likely to have a hand in.

Control is a process of ensuring that an organisation's goals are achieved, that procedures are adhered to, and that an organisation responds appropriately to changes in its environment.

There are three primary types of organisational control:

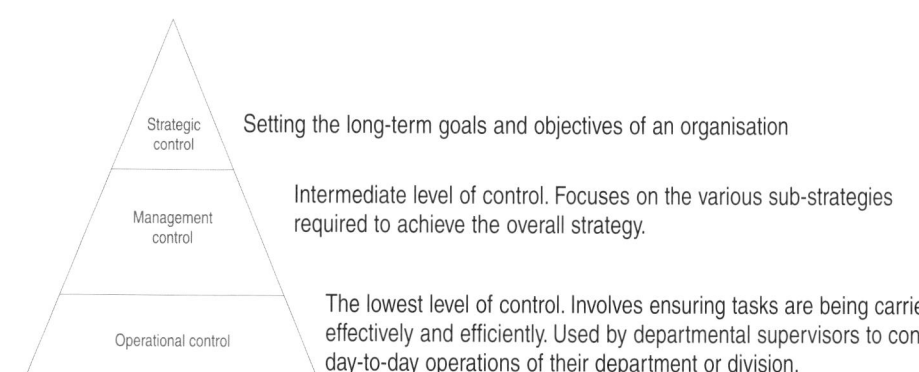

Strategic control — Setting the long-term goals and objectives of an organisation

Management control — Intermediate level of control. Focuses on the various sub-strategies required to achieve the overall strategy.

Operational control — The lowest level of control. Involves ensuring tasks are being carried out effectively and efficiently. Used by departmental supervisors to control the day-to-day operations of their department or division.

Return on investment (ROI)

This is a form of return on capital employed

$$\frac{\text{Profit before interest and tax}}{\text{Operations management capital employed}} \times 100$$

Advantages	Disadvantages
<ul><li>Easy to prepare</li><li>Takes many aspects into account</li><li>Shows percentage rather than absolute value, so can compare divisions of different sizes.</li></ul>	<ul><li>Vulnerable to manipulation</li><li>Does not look at cash flow</li><li>Managers have an incentive not to invest, so may encourage short-termism</li><li>More suited to mature product-market phase</li></ul>

Residual income (RI)

This is a measure of the centre's profits **after deducting an imputed interest cost**. RI will increase when investments are made that have returns higher than the firm's cost of capital. Cost of capital can be varied according to the risk characteristics of different investments.

Comparing profit centres

Problems

- They do not always pursue goal congruence
- They share resources
- They often work with and for each other
- How are overheads to be absorbed?

Measures of performance

- Contribution
- Controllable profit
- Controllable margin
- Net profit, after a charge
- Added value

Solution?

Treat them as investment centres and levy a management charge

Interfirm comparisons

eg for benchmarking, or comparing subsidiaries

Problems

- Assessing capital employed
- Accounting policies
- Different ways of financing growth
- Tax rates

Measures

- Normal accounting ratios
- Information about cost structures
- Profitability
- Financial structure
- Cash flows

A shareholder value approach to performance measurement moves the focus away from short term profits to a longer term view of value creation.

Different shareholders will value different aspects of performance, although they will generally prioritise **financial returns**.

Shareholder value analysis (SVA)

Rappaport's seven value drivers

- Sales growth rate
- Operating profit margin
- Fixed capital investment
- Working capital investment   } all driving cash generation
- Cash tax rate
- The planning period
- The cost of capital

The development of SVA has been driven by:

- Wider share ownership
- More knowledgeable investors
- Desire to get away from a short term outlook
- Discrediting of profit as the sole performance measure

We need to ask the question: **How well is the business performing for the shareholder?**

Shareholder value = (business value – debt)

where business value equals PV of free cashflows from operations plus the value of any marketable assets held

Economic value management

EVA = Adjusted operating profits after tax − (Adjusted invested capital × imputed rate of interest)

This hinges on the calculation of **economic profit (EP)**, which avoids the immediate write-off of value-building expenditure such as R&D or training. This produces a figure for **economic value added or destroyed.**

→ produces →

A figure for **capital employed** which is a more accurate reflection of:

1. Basis for shareholders' returns

2. Cash yield generated from recurring business activities

3. Investment in assets

Value based management

A managerial process which links strategy, measurement and operational processes to the end of creating shareholder value.

Developed in response to criticisms of profit-based measures such as ROI or RI.

Other measures

- **Market value added**: the difference between a company's *market value* and the *book value* of capital employed

- **Total shareholder return:**

$$\frac{\text{Dividend per share + Movement in share price}}{\text{Share price at the start of the period}}$$

Setting objectives within a multinational is a complex task. There are particular difficulties with performance measurement when operations and functions are located in various parts of the world.

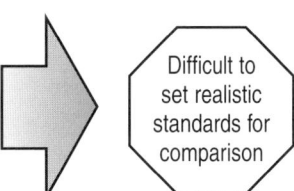

Problems to be resolved

- Capital structure and interest rates
- Cost structure
- Accounting policies
- Government policy (eg tax rates)
- Transfer prices
- Exchange rate fluctuations
- Risk
- Domestic competition
- Economic conditions/infrastructure
- Management control and staffing
- Cultural differences

Difficult to set realistic standards for comparison

Transfer prices are made to account for the transfers of goods/services between one department or division to another.

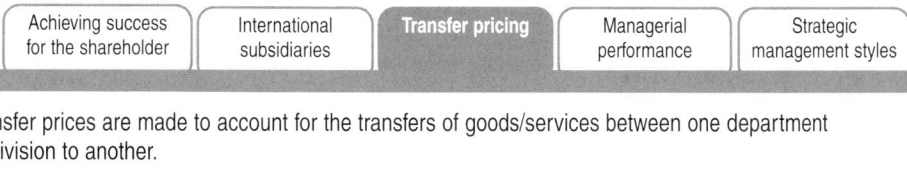

Principles

Ensure goal congruence
Do not use as penalty/reward

Uses

- Track the cost of work in progress
- Allocate profits to internal departments

Levels

- Marginal cost
- Full cost with mark-up
- Market price
- Negotiated price

Negotiations needed when:

- The best price cannot be calculated
- There is an element of risk
- Authority is decentralised and disputes arise

Eccles says the method of setting transfer prices should reflect the organisation's degree of diversification and vertical integration.

The basic principle to remember here is that managers should only be assesed on what they can **control**.

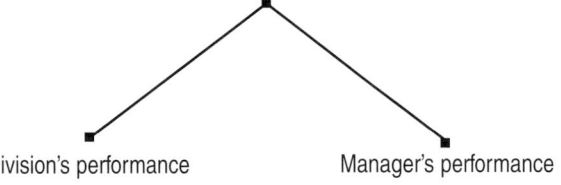

Division's performance   Manager's performance

Example: A company has three operating divisions and a head office.

In order to evaluate the performance of the three divisional **managers**, the share of indirect costs re-apportioned from the head office should not be included – because the divisional manager cannot control them.

But, in order to evaluate the **division's** overall performance, it is appropriate to include a share of head office costs. If the divisions were independent companies they would have to incur the cost of those services currently provided through the head office (eg finance and HR costs).

Reward systems

Rewarding managers for their performance is a method of control that assumes that managers will attempt to achieve the organisation's objectives in return for rewards. But there are problems with this:

- Different individuals value different types of reward
- The value of a reward may be affected by external factors
- Managers may not want to wait for their reward
- Rewards may encourage short-termist thinking and manipulation

Incentive schemes (PRP, bonuses)

Assume that people are at least partly motivated by financial reward

BUT

Not always the case. Status and personal satisfaction, for example, are also important.

Typical features

- Payments related to controllable factors
- Clear and fair calculation
- Flexible
- Sometimes long term, (eg share options)
- Often short term (eg based on profitability)

3 main roles for the corporate centre

1 Determination of overall strategy and allocation of resources

2 Controlling divisional performance

3 Providing central services (eg HR, legal)

Strategic management styles (Goold & Campbell)

Strategic planning style: Centre heavily involved in strategic planning: lots of dialogue between centre and divisions. Centre less involved in control than planning, and does not impose rigid targets on divisions. Performance targets focus on longer-term strategic objectives.

Strategic control: Fairly low amount of planning influence from centre but tight control.

Financial control: Centre takes little interest in strategy and strategic decisions, and company will not have a formal long-term strategy. Strategic discussions revolve around annual budget process, and corporate centre exercises control through budgets and profit targets.

Notes

14: Enterprise performance management

Topic List

Control systems

Financial and non-financial measures

Multidimensional measures

Services and manufacturing

Performance measurement aims to

- *Communicate the objectives of the company*
- *Concentrate efforts towards those objectives*
- *Provide feedback and control of the plan*

There need to be systems for strategic control, featuring strategy review, performance milestones and target achievement levels.

A major function of organisation structure is the provision of a mechanism through which control can be exercised. A feedback or cybernetic control system works like this.

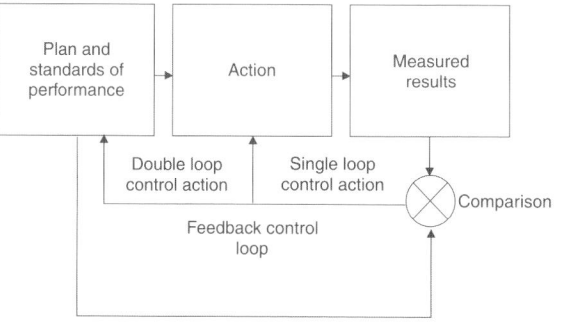

Ouchi has identified 3 types of control

- **Market control** assigns revenues and costs to profit centres and control is exercised via financial performance. It works well with autonomous trading units but not for centrally provided services.

- **Bureaucratic control** uses formal structures and procedures. It is impersonal, rational and efficient but relies on objective measurement. It is less useful where subjective impressions are important (eg where outputs are difficult to measure).

- **Cultural or clan control** works through shaping values, attitudes and commitment. It is useful for complex, abstruse or highly specialised work (such as research) where outputs are difficult to measure or to price.

A budget is a plan expressed in monetary terms

Purposes of budgets

- To compel planning
- To co-ordinate activities
- To communicate ideas
- To provide a framework for responsibility accounting
- To motivate employees/management
- To evaluate performance

Budgetary control is a control system using budgets to ensure the achievement of objectives and results.

Elements of a budgeting system

- How the information is presented
- Who receives the information
- What information? eg
  - timescale?
  - detail/format?
- Budgeting techniques, eg
  - flexed budget?
  - rolling budget?
  - ABB/ZBB
- Comparisons made, eg
  - budget v actual
  - variance analysis
  - competition

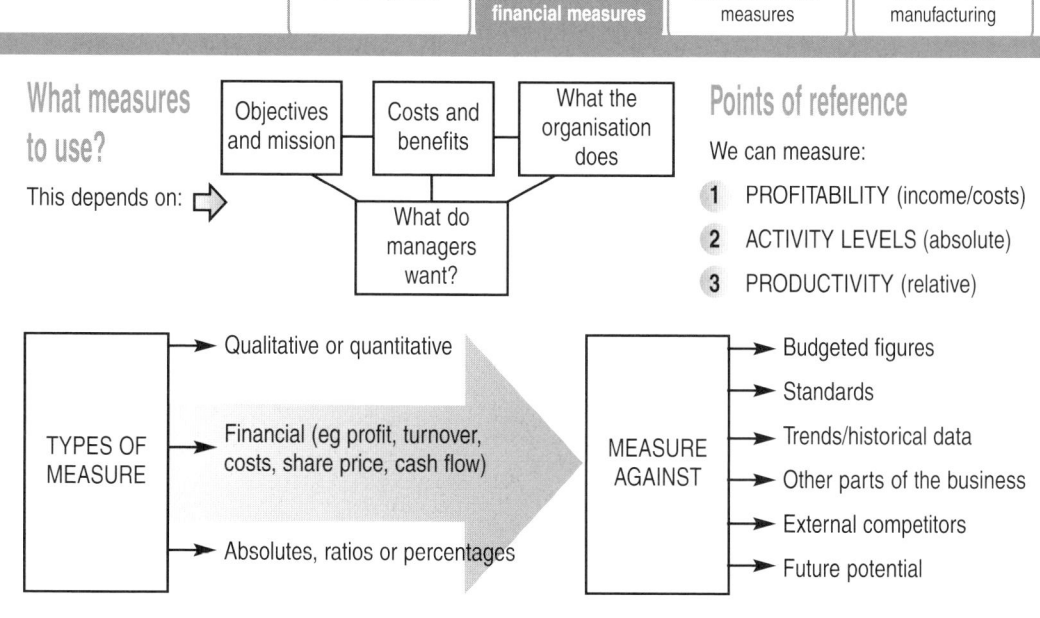

What measures to use?

This depends on: ➡

- Objectives and mission
- Costs and benefits
- What the organisation does
- What do managers want?

Points of reference

We can measure:

1. PROFITABILITY (income/costs)
2. ACTIVITY LEVELS (absolute)
3. PRODUCTIVITY (relative)

TYPES OF MEASURE
- ➤ Qualitative or quantitative
- ➤ Financial (eg profit, turnover, costs, share price, cash flow)
- ➤ Absolutes, ratios or percentages

MEASURE AGAINST
- ➤ Budgeted figures
- ➤ Standards
- ➤ Trends/historical data
- ➤ Other parts of the business
- ➤ External competitors
- ➤ Future potential

Examples

FINANCIAL MEASURES	NON-FINANCIAL MEASURES
Working capital ratios	Market share trends
Cash flow	Growth of customer numbers
EPS	Customer returns
Share price	Enquiries
Variance analysis	Customer satisfaction
Revenue targets	Late deliveries
Customer profitability analysis	Quality
Profit and margins	Labour turnover
ROI and RI	Labour skills
Wastage	Production performance
Inventory turnover	Innovation

A combination of the two types is best.

Critical success factors (CSFs)

are those actions that must be performed well in order for the goals and objectives of an organisation to be met successfully

Once an organisation has identified which areas it needs to perform well in, its performance in these areas must be measured. Therefore, one or more key performance indicators (KPIs) have to be established for each CSF.

Key performance indicators (KPIs)

are the **measures** which indicate whether or not the CSFs are being achieved

Exam focus

Make sure you appreciate the difference between CSFs and KPIs. CSFs indicate what must be done well to enable an organisation to be successful (eg producing high quality goods). KPIs are the measures of whether or not these CSFs are being achieved and so must be measurable (eg number of defects in production).

Traditional accounting measures are inadequate for assessing overall progress. Other matters must be considered, especially as financial reporting is heavily retrospective in focus. The **balanced scorecard** covers most of the angles with its four **perspectives**. Note that individual measures are **company specific.**

Customer perspective

'How should we appear to customers?' This perspective concentrates on customers' concern with time, quality, performance and service. Example measures would be percentage of on-time deliveries and customer rejection rates.

Internal business perspective

'What must we excel at?' This perspective focuses on what the company must be internally to meet its customers' expectations. Control measures will focus on core competences, skills, productivity and cost, for example.

Innovation and learning perspective

'Can we continue to improve and create value?' This perspective is forward looking and concentrates on what the company must do to satisfy future needs. Performance measures include time-to-market for new products and percentage of revenue from them.

Financial perspective

'How do we create value for shareholders?' This is the traditional reporting perspective, but must not be overlooked. Market share and sales growth are included here. Modern measures like value-added and shareholder value analysis should be included.

14: Enterprise performance management

Possible indicators for balanced scorecard categories:

Customer perspective
■ Market share
■ Number of new customers attracted
■ Number of recommendations or referrals
■ Customer satisfaction ratings
■ Customer retention rates
■ Levels of refunds/returns
■ % of deliveries on time

Internal business perspective
■ Reduced inventory levels
■ Reduced lead times
■ Delivery dates of new products in line with plan
■ Minimise wastage/errors
■ Reliability and usability (of websites)
■ Security of transactions and credit card handling

Innovation and learning
■ New products/processes developed
■ Time to market for new products
■ % of sales from new products
■ Number of new products developed (vs competitors)
■ Ideas from employees
■ Reward and recognition structure for staff

Financial perspective
■ Turnover or operating profit
■ Asset utilisation
■ Market share
■ ROI; EVA
■ Cashflow

Implementing the balanced scorecard

Kaplan & Norton recommend a four stage approach:

1. Express organisation's mission in a way that has clear operational meaning for each employee.

2. Link mission to departmental or individual objectives, (not confined to short-term financial goals).

3. Use scorecard to prioritise objectives and allocate resources so as to make best progress towards strategic goals.

4. Use feedback on performance to promote progress against the four perspectives.

Words of warning

Possible problems when applying the scorecard:

- Some measures may conflict – how do you determine the balance which achieves the best results?

- Have to select measures which add value, not just those that are easy to measure

- Measures have to be developed by someone who understands the business processes involved.

- Will management be able to interpret the figures, or will they just be swamped in a mass of figures? To be useful, measurement needs to initiate action to improve performance.

- There will be a cost involved in measuring the performance of additional processes to those that are currently measured.

The performance pyramid

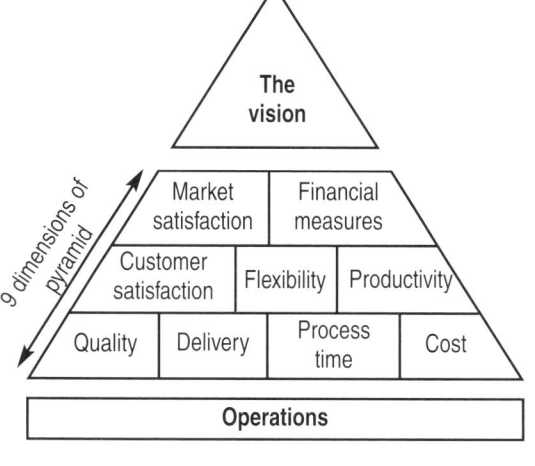

Building block model

Results	■ Competitive performance ■ Financial performance
Determinants of those results	■ Quality of service ■ Flexibility ■ Resource utilisation ■ Innovation
■ Standards	■ Employees must take ownership ■ Achievable ■ Fair
■ Rewards	■ Clarity ■ Provide motivation ■ Controllability

Service departments and firms

Service departments control exercised via			Firms

Service departments control exercised via

- Budgeting
- Deadlines
- Performance measures
- Profit
- Quality targets

$$\text{Efficiency} = \frac{\text{units of activity}}{\text{units of resource}}$$

Firms

Building block model (results and determinants)

Key questions for management:

- How is the department using up the organisations resources?
- What is the department costing?
- Could the department improve efficiency and reduce costs?

14: Enterprise performance management

Manufacturing

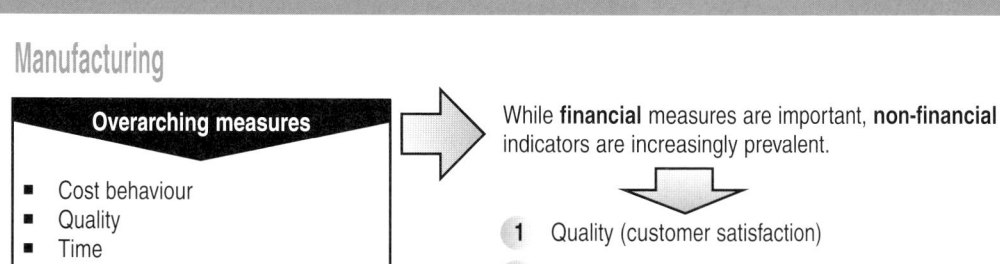

Overarching measures

- Cost behaviour
- Quality
- Time
- Innovation

While **financial** measures are important, **non-financial** indicators are increasingly prevalent.

1. Quality (customer satisfaction)
2. Delivery (fast and reliable)
3. Capacity utilisation/productivity
4. Flexibility

Notes

Notes

Notes

Notes